MOTHER TERESA'S PRESCRIPTION

MOTHER TERESA'S PRESCRIPTION

Finding HAPPINESS and PEACE in SERVICE

PAUL A. WRIGHT, M.D.

Ave Maria Press Notre Dame, Indiana

All royalties from this book are being freely donated to the Missionaries of Charity to continue Mother Teresa's work of serving the poor.

Founded in 1865, Ave Maria Press is a ministry of the United States Province of Holy Cross.

www.avemariapress.com

ISBN-10 1-59471-072-4 ISBN-13 978-1-59471-072-8

Cover and text design by John Carson

Photos: front cover, page 18, page 58 ©AP/Wide World Photos; other photos courtesy of author.

Printed and bound in the United States of America.

Library of Congress Cataloging-in-Publication Data

Wright, Paul A., 1950-

Mother Teresa's prescription : finding happiness and peace in service / Paul A. Wright.

p. cm.

Includes bibliographical references.

ISBN-13: 978-1-59471-072-8 (pbk.)

ISBN-10: 1-59471-072-4 (pbk.)

1. Service (Theology) 2. Christian life. 3. Contentment--Religious aspects--Christianity. 4. Teresa, Mother, 1910- 5. Happiness--Religious aspects--Christianity. 6. Peace--Religious aspects--Christianity. I. Title.

BT738.4.W75 2006
248.4'82--dc22

2005027498

Dedication and Acknowledgments

I dedicate this book to the memory of Blessed Mother Teresa of Calcutta for the way in which she changed my life and the lives of countless others,

To all the Missionaries of Charity,

To my family, especially my daughter Maria Alana,

And to the memory of my uncle and aunt, Frank and Theresa Davis.

My special thanks to Donna M. Davis for the time and effort she dedicated to organizing and editing this book. I would also like to acknowledge Susan K. Virgalitte for helping in the planning stages of the project.

TABLE OF CONTENTS

UNIVERSITY OF
NOTRE DAME

REV. THEODORE M. HESBURGH, C.S.C.
President Emeritus

1315 Hesburgh Library
Notre Dame, Indiana
46556-5629 USA

Telephone (574) 631-6882
Facsimile (574) 631-6877
E-mail Theodore.M.Hesburgh.1@nd.edu

Paul A. Wright, M.D.
7171 Sunnydell Drive
Brookfield, Ohio 44403

Dear Paul,

I believe the best blessings upon this book, *Mother Teresa's Prescription*, that one might request of the Good Lord is to have Him not only bless it Himself but also to include the blessing of Mother Teresa which is what this book is all about. Mother Teresa, just by being what she was, is indeed a blessing on all of the Church.

A short comment on this work... I believe that Mother Teresa was one of the greatest persons who lived in the last century. Had I the power, I would have canonized her the day she closed her eyes and died. It was fantastic to see all of those leaders of Eastern religions spending hours celebrating her life and her death. I cannot think of any Christian who has ever received this kind of acceptance from the Muslims, Hindus, Buddhists and Shintos and all of the rest of the religious who flourish in the Orient.

One of the lasting blessings of great people is that their work goes on through others whom they inspire. The author of this work spent five years learning those lessons from Mother Teresa, and his work, I am sure, is very pleasing to her. In a very real sense, it is a continuation of what she did on earth. This book presents many of Mother Teresa's own great spiritual ideas and ideals and inspires other people to go on doing the work she did so well on earth. One can only bless this work and pray for its total prosperity in the days to come.

We also ask the Holy Spirit to bless all those who continue the work that this book describes and to bring them blessings in their own lives.

Ever devotedly in Notre Dame,

Rev. Theodore M. Hesburgh, C.S.C.
President Emeritus
July 26, 2005

Foreword

I first heard Paul Wright's account of his life-transforming encounter with Mother Teresa of Calcutta a decade or so ago. He related it to an audience of Notre Dame alumni physicians and medical ethics experts in McKenna Hall at Notre Dame's annual medical ethics conference. In an abbreviated form, Paul Wright shared the account he tells here. I was moved then by his telling of this story, and I have been moved once again in reading it.

I told him on that occasion that this story should be shared with more people. Since then, many others have encouraged him to publish it. Happily, we now have his book for all to read.

It is a remarkable journey, a journey like some of the great spiritual classics—a quest and a life transformed in that quest. Dr. Wright finds himself in the midst of a successful life, a life marked by a flourishing career, a wonderful family, abundant material goods, financial security, and a respected role in the community. His is a good life by all the measures we conventionally apply to lives in contemporary culture. At the heart of his outwardly successful life, however, he discovers dissatisfaction and emptiness. His unhappiness motivates his search for an answer to the question none of us can ultimately avoid—What is the purpose of my life? By what standards will I be judged at the end of this life?

His book tells of the quest to answer that question, an answer he finally arrives at with the assistance of Mother Teresa. Like the rich young man who comes to Jesus to ask what he must do to be saved, Dr. Wright seeks out a living saint, Mother Teresa, for help in answering this question.

Dr. Wright's quest takes him to Tijuana, Calcutta, Rome, and to a number of places of Christian hospitality in this country. But the external journey he takes is less important than his internal journey into the self. This book is a *vade mecum* (guidebook) of the spiritual life, inviting the reader to accompany Dr. Wright on a journey all must travel if they are to be truly human. It is a journey of self-discovery as well as a journey of ethical and personal commitment.

Dr. Wright seems surprised at points in this story by the simplicity of Mother Teresa's advice. For a question that has such momentous import for his life, he seems to think that one should have a grand and complex answer. But the answer is simplicity itself—love and compassion is what is required of us. While the lesson he is taught is simple, it is not easy. Genuine love and compassion are demanding requirements. They require nothing short of the transformation of self—a transformation especially difficult for a successful and properly ambitious modern man like Paul Wright.

Among the most difficult lessons for Dr. Wright, one senses, is Mother Teresa's insistence that genuine love and compassion do not require that he fly off to exotic places like Tijuana and Calcutta to exercise his love. Instead, it would mean that he should stay at home, in Youngstown, Ohio. Charity, in a real sense, must begin at home.

We can all be grateful, I think, that Dr. Wright is not a professional philosopher or theologian. He writes about the most important issues of personal conduct with a directness and clarity that one seldom finds in academic writing. I have seen the impact his story has had on mature physicians as well as on Notre Dame undergraduates. We can all be grateful that this story will now reach a much wider audience. Dr. Wright has worked with great energy in the last decade on programs to respond to the needs of "Christ in the distressing disguise of the poor." I suspect, however, that his greatest service to all of us may be this honest and profound account of transformations in his own life.

David Solomon, Ph.D.
Director, Center for Ethics and Culture
University of Notre Dame
August 22, 2005

Introduction

I am a physician, a healer by profession. Over the past two decades, I have written thousands of prescriptions to help support, sustain, and heal my patients' cardiovascular systems. Treating the sick has brought me much personal fulfillment and satisfaction, as well as material success. In 1992, however, I realized something was missing from my life. It was that sense of inner peace and happiness that so many of us are seeking. I constantly felt stressed, short on time, impatient, and dissatisfied. My focus had become attaining ever-increasing amounts of control, power, wealth, and prestige even though they brought me no joy. At the same time, I was haunted by the thought that I was not doing well in God's eyes despite my efforts to lead a good life and be a compassionate physician. I kept asking myself why God had put me on earth. What was my purpose in life? I could find no answer, no prescription for healing. The one patient I could not cure was myself—until I sought out Mother Teresa of Calcutta. I considered her to be the expert on living the Christian life.

Our first meeting took place in February 1992 in Tijuana, Mexico, at a homeless shelter run by her order, the Missionaries of Charity. It was there that I heard Mother's message about the purpose of life. I am convinced that God arranged that meeting, not only for my sake but also for everyone who would hear my story. That initial forty-five minute encounter led to many others. Our relationship lasted until her death in 1997 and took me first to Mexico, and then to Calcutta, India, to the motherhouse of the Missionaries of Charity. I visited their orphanages, leprosy colonies, and the House of the Dying. This friendship also took me to Jenkins, Kentucky, in the heart of Appalachia, to soup kitchens and homeless shelters in Harlem and the Bronx and to an AIDS house in Washington, D.C. Later, it also led me to St. Peter's Square in Rome, and always back to my hometown of Youngstown, Ohio. Along the way, I experienced confusion, rejection, and even humiliation. With Mother Teresa's guidance, however, I discovered my purpose in life, and with it, her prescription for inner peace and happiness and the healing for humanity. Now, I want to share that prescription with you.

This book explains how Mother Teresa taught me about the purpose of life and her prescription for its healing, which is based on the teachings of Jesus Christ. Following the prescription means embracing the true purpose of life and the ten attitudes of spirit that go along with it: compassion and love, contentment and gratitude, honesty, patience, tolerance, forgiveness, humility, commitment to community, faith, and reverence for human life. Mother Teresa embodied all of these qualities. I heard her message about the purpose of life, and then I observed her at work to discern the ten attitudes I needed to add to my life.

The life story of the woman now formally known as Blessed Teresa of Calcutta is familiar to many of us—how she began ministering to people dying on the streets of Calcutta in 1952 and founded a religious order, the Missionaries of Charity, which now serves the "poorest of the poor" in more than five hundred missions in over a hundred countries. I do not attempt to repeat that history but to tell instead the story of what I learned from Mother Teresa. Perhaps it can help others who are dealing with the same spiritual malady I faced.

In the years before her death, I came to view Mother Teresa as my physician. As a cardiologist, I sometimes monitored her blood pressure and supplied her with various cardiovascular medications. But I did not heal her. Instead, I became her patient and she became my spiritual physician. She healed me.

54A, A.J.C. BOSE ROAD, CALCUTTA-700016

"As long as you did it to one of these My least brethren. You did it to Me"

1st. December'94

To
The Deputy Commn. of Police,
F.R.R.O. (Security Control)
237, A.J.C. Bose Road,
Calcutta

Dear Mr. Tapas,

I, Mother M. Teresa m.c. hereby Certify that Dr. Paul Wright and American National and one of our Missionaries of Chatiy Co-worker, holder of Passport bearing No.083755642 issued in New Orleans on 17-6-94 and valid till 16-6-2004, has come to India to handover the Medicines for me.

There was no time for him to obtain the necessary VISA, hence he travelled without any, but the Consul General of India, Mr. S.N. Ray had advised him to travel to India immediately, hence he came on 28-11-94 at C.A.P.

His Passport was taken away at the Security Counter and he was told to collect the same from your Office.

I shall be grateful if you will handover his Passport today as he needs the same for change of money and other formalities. He will be leaving India on AIR INDIA on Saturday the 3rd. December, 1994.

Thanking you, for your kind concern and I assure you of my prayers always.

Encl: Copy letter of
Consul (S.N.RAY)

God bless you
M Teresa mc

Now, I believe Mother Teresa would want me to make that healing advice available to others. I invite you to follow me as I tell you a little about my spiritual healing and how you can apply Mother's therapy to your life, no matter who you are or what you do. I have also included questions for you to consider, either for your personal journey or for group discussion. You may want to keep a journal as you move through this book. Go slowly. You cannot "take" the entire prescription overnight. You may want to try adding each spiritual attitude one at a time, over weeks, months, or even years.

I will be honest. Undertaking this spiritual therapy is not easy. It is not a formula for sainthood—few of us are called, as Mother Teresa was, to that special life. Her prescriptions, however, do require commitment and the understanding that some people, including close friends and family members, may be confused or even alienated by your new life. Once undertaken, this healthy new life will help you grow in love and compassion. It will give you the means to move from a mindset of frustration, anger, and self-centeredness to one of inner peace and sustainable happiness. Most important, Mother's prescription will empower you to discover and pursue God's unique purpose for your life.

Included in this introduction is a copy of a personal letter from Mother Teresa to the Deputy Commissioner of Police in Calcutta asking the Security Control to return my passport so that I could leave India and return home. This letter reminds me of the many things that Blessed Mother Teresa did to facilitate my spiritual journey. At the end of the book, as Appendix material, I have also included a listing of the houses of the Missionaries of Charity in North America. Perhaps you can get to know the wonderful men and women who are part of this order and find inspiration in their work for your life and work. There is also information about the Thomas A. Dooley Award, an award given for humanitarian service by the Alumnae Association of the University of Notre Dame. I was given this award in 2004, but information about this is not included to promote my own reputation. It is to show that all of us can find unique ways to serve, giving our gifts and time to those who need it most. I found mine and I hope that—with Mother Teresa's prescription—you may find yours.

Peace be with you,

Paul A. Wright, M.D.
Youngstown, Ohio

PART 1 Mother's Message

CHAPTER 1 Something Missing

In 1992 I was enjoying the life of the successful American doctor. At the age of forty, I was a respected cardiologist, known throughout northeastern Ohio and western Pennsylvania. My partners and I had built a huge new facility that we envisioned as a regional state-of-the-art center for treating patients with cardiovascular disease. My personal life was just as fulfilling. My wife, Gayle, and I were happily raising our eleven-year-old daughter, Maria Alana. The three of us were excitedly going forward with plans to build a huge, costly dream home in an affluent neighborhood. Despite the long hours I worked, I also devoted time and money to community activities and local charities. To the outside world, everything looked perfect and complete. Yet something was missing from my life.

In spite of everything I had, all that I had accomplished, I still had not achieved my ultimate goal in life: inner peace and happiness. As my medical practice grew, so did my stress. Satisfying my expectations and the expectations of my partners, employees, hospital administrators, insurance companies, even family and friends, consumed all my time. Everyone wanted something from me. Even though I willingly supplied what they needed, I did not feel happy or at peace. Instead, pangs of insecurity, restlessness, and dissatisfaction nagged me. I continued to question why I was here. What was my true purpose in life? What was the purpose of humanity? Finally, I concluded that I had misdirected my mental and physical energies. I could find the answers I needed not in the world of materialism and power, but in the spiritual world. I needed a closer connection to God and a way to be a success in his eyes, not just those of my partners and associates. How could I achieve that connection and find the way to happiness and inner peace?

My restlessness grew as the worry that I had actually accomplished nothing for humanity overwhelmed me. I wondered how God saw me and how he would ultimately judge me. To others, I appeared to be a successful, healthy, and productive person with a gift for healing. But inside, I was not at peace with the world or myself. What would it take to find that peace? Who could help me?

As a physician, I believed—and still do believe—that there must be some prescription or antidote to heal or at least improve almost any condition. So I followed the advice any physician would give to a patient suffering from a complicated illness. I sought out a specialist. It seemed logical that if I suffered from a spiritual malady, I should consult the person most capable of answering my questions about the purpose of life and how God would judge me. I wanted someone who would answer my questions as perfectly as anyone could.

I began to look for that person, and the name that I kept encountering was that of Mother Teresa of Calcutta. For years, her name had been synonymous with the term "living saint," the only one I had ever heard of. I wanted to see what a living saint looked like. I wanted to feel her hands on my face and look into her eyes. Who else but a living saint would so perfectly embody the true purpose of life? She certainly would have answers to "Why am I here, and what is my God-given responsibility to others?" I needed to find out what motivated her, what gave her a purpose for living. How had she achieved such inner peace and happiness? Finally, I wanted to hear how

Paul Wright met Mother Teresa for the first time on February 1, 1992, at a center for the homeless run by her Missionaries of Charity in Tijuana, Mexico. A tired-looking, unengaged Mother Teresa was recovering from a recent heart attack.

she would answer the most burning question in my heart: How would God judge me at the moment of my death?

If Mother Teresa was a living saint—someone many people considered a perfect human being—then certainly the service she gave to the sick and dying was something we should all be doing. Still I had to ask myself three questions: Why did she give such wholehearted and selfless service to the sick and dying in such terrible conditions? Could I practice medicine under similar circumstances? Did God require me to do so?

These questions stayed in my mind and drove me to seek a personal, private discussion with Mother Teresa. Reading articles about her work, her philosophy, and her spirituality were no longer enough. Nor did I want to seek advice from other, substitute spiritual advisers who might be more easily accessible to me. I wanted to hear Mother Teresa's message coming personally from her to me. I wanted to hear her voice directed at me. Only then would I believe, understand, and accept. That is why on February 1, 1992, I found myself walking toward a small homeless shelter operated by Mother Teresa's Missionaries of Charity in Tijuana, Mexico.

SOMETHING TO CONSIDER . . .

1. What are the sources of confusion or lack of fulfillment in your life?
2. Where do you look for inspiration, for comfort?
3. Who is the person you would most like to emulate? Why? What qualities in this person attract you?

CHAPTER 2 First Encounter

I stood before the locked gate of the small cement building that housed the Beato Juan Diego shelter, not knowing when the nuns who ran the shelter would allow me to come inside. Mother Teresa of Calcutta and her sisters were at prayer, and during that time of private devotion, they admitted no visitors.

Instead of the typical tourist garb of flip-flops, shorts, and T-shirt or the baggy, comfortable scrubs I wore at work, I had put on my best summer suit, a white shirt, a tie, and dress shoes. I hoped to look my most professional and well groomed best. Within moments, though, I was soaking wet from the heat and humidity. As the minutes passed, I thought about how I had arrived here, hundreds of miles from my home and busy practice in wintry northeast Ohio.

The trip had been a brash, spur-of-the-moment move, driven mostly by my spiritual pain and my desperation to find answers to my questions. A few days before, Gayle and my mother, aware of my quest, had shown me a newspaper article that said Mother Teresa was somewhere in Tijuana recuperating from heart problems. I knew that the Missionaries of Charity had a homeless shelter in Tijuana. On a hunch, I telephoned and talked to Sister Sabina, the superior. She told me that Mother Teresa was indeed resting at the Beato Juan Diego shelter. When I explained that I absolutely needed to see

Mother Teresa to ask her some questions, Sister Sabina said that Mother was not yet well enough for visitors. "Call back in a few days if you still desire an interview," she said. Several days later, I did make that second call, and Sister Sabina informed me that Mother would be pleased to see me.

A full half-hour passed before one of the sisters unlocked the gate and led me through a small screen door and into a narrow corridor, where Sister Sabina greeted me.

"Please spend some time with the Master of the house," she said as she showed me into the clinic's small chapel. I removed my shoes, as is the custom in all Missionaries of Charity homes. I then knelt before the large crucifix and began to pray.

My heart was pounding as I asked God to give me the strength to face Mother Teresa and to admit my spiritual weakness. I prayed that this busy woman, this living saint, would not reject me. I feared that she might dismiss me as a pampered, wealthy American who was taking her away from her mission to serve the poor. Still, I hoped that somehow she would give me the guidance—even just a few words—that I so needed and answer my question: How would God judge me? So I waited.

After another thirty minutes, one of the sisters escorted me from the chapel to a small room furnished only with a wooden desk and two small chairs. There was no air conditioning, and I continued to sweat profusely in the unbearable heat. So much for the perfectly groomed professional! Someone must have noticed my discomfort because a sister brought me a glass of water. Then the door opened and Mother Teresa, wearing sandals and the familiar white sari trimmed in blue, walked into the room.

"How frail and tiny she looks," I thought. I am five feet six inches tall, but I towered over her as I stood to greet her.

I could see that she was very tired. She walked slowly and shuffled slightly as she moved toward the chair and sat down.

My initial surprise at Mother Teresa's physical appearance was quickly replaced with joy at finally being in her presence.

She placed her hands on the wooden table with her palms up. I did the same. The table was so small that my hands could have easily touched hers, but I did not dare make contact.

She skipped the usual introductions and pleasantries and simply smiled at me and asked, "Why did you come?"

I told her I wanted to see what a perfect human being looked like in person. I wanted to look into the eyes of someone so full of love and compassion. I wanted to touch the hands of a woman so close to God.

Mother Teresa lifted her hands toward me. I stood up slightly and leaned forward as she placed a hand on each side of my face. Instantly, I felt a sense of peace and serenity that I had not experienced since childhood. She truly had a mother's touch. I burst into tears, an unusual reaction for me. I quickly regained my composure and sat down. I was a little embarrassed by my outburst, yet I felt calm and relaxed.

I told her I desperately needed a stronger focus and understanding of God's purpose for my life. If I understood what criteria God would use to judge me, then I would have a better understanding of my purpose.

Then I asked my question—the one that had been burning in my heart for so long.

"Mother, can you tell me how Jesus will judge me at the moment of my death?"

Mother Teresa smiled again and nodded "yes." She rose, went to the door, and asked one of the sisters to bring her a bible.

I could tell Mother Teresa was delighted with my question. As we waited, she explained that the answer to my question was the very foundation and purpose of her Missionaries of Charity. Then she took the bible and immediately opened it to chapter 25 of the Gospel of Matthew. "In the bible, there is one place where Jesus describes how he will judge all nations, all people," she said.

The bible lay open in front of us, but Mother Teresa did not read from it. The story was one she had told so many people, so many times, and as she looked straight at me and spoke, I felt I was the only person she had ever shared it with.

"Jesus said when he comes to judge, he will separate all people into two groups, just as the shepherd separates the sheep from the goats. And Jesus will say to those on his right, 'You shall enter the Kingdom of Glory because when I was hungry, you fed me; when I was naked, you clothed me; when I was thirsty, you gave me drink; when I was sick, you tended to me.' And those on the right will say, 'But, Lord, when did I see you naked or hungry or thirsty?'"

Then Mother Teresa took my hand. "Jesus said whatever you do for the least of our brothers and sisters," and touching one of my fingers with each word, she concluded, "you . . . did . . . it . . . to . . . me."

God will judge us on how we loved and how much compassion we had for our brothers and sisters, she told me. Her order recognizes that Jesus "comes to us in the distressing disguise of the poor" and asks for our help. She explained that I would not be judged by how much money I earned, how many titles I had beside my name, how much power I possessed, or how many buildings I owned, but by how much sincere compassion I gave to others, especially the poor. She did not know that I was a physician nor did she ask any questions about my religion or my profession. Those issues did not matter to her. All she saw was a person in need of her message of love and compassion.

I had mixed feelings as I listened to her words. On the one hand, I felt pleased that I had received the wisdom that would give perfect purpose to my life. But I also realized that such a calling would require a real transformation. I would have to reject my materialistic, competitive mindset and focus on becoming someone chiefly concerned with alleviating the suffering of others, without regard for personal reward. My affirmation of the purpose of life is only possible when I give myself away for another life. The only investment I needed to worry about was not on Wall Street. Instead, I would invest myself in serving others with compassion. I would invest my humanity to serve humanity.

I understand now that in this first meeting with Mother Teresa I had hoped she would tell me that I was doing fine. I thought she would assure me that I was leading a good, Christian life, but to try to be a bit more generous with my time and money and a little less impatient with patients, colleagues, and others. Her diagnosis, however, was much more honest and accurate. She had recognized me as spiritually needy. My gut feeling had been correct. I was falling short; I did not understand God's purpose for me.

Achieving the true purpose that Mother Teresa had laid out before me through the words of Jesus would not be easy. I knew, however, that I had found my long-sought purpose of life. This wisdom did not reveal itself through human logic or reason, or through degrees or academic excellence. My previous motivations had failed me. A concept that would have sounded so illogical to me days earlier—that material goods and prestige are not the avenues to happiness—now made perfect sense. I would have to focus on the new motivation she had given me.

This was the moment of my epiphany and the beginning of my transformation. I now realized clearly that the purpose of life is bound to self-sacrifice and the responsibility to serve humanity and God within humanity. The single, correct motivation must be compassion, that is, to alleviate the suffering of others, especially the poor. My personal affirmation of the purpose of life, as Mother Teresa explained to me, would be to give myself to others. I had always desired to resolve suffering, but now I realized it should be my primary motivation. I needed to start seeing the purpose of my life as not doing something to accomplish or acquire *something*, but to always be doing something for *someone*, as Mother Teresa did.

I also knew that I would have to accept the consequences of that change in my outlook. Putting this understanding into action would mean altering my thinking and my principle motivations. Mother Teresa often said that for an act to be of value, compassion should be the motivating force. I could be examining a patient, treating that patient extremely well, and the patient could progress well medically. But I would not serve my true purpose in life unless my primary motivation was compassion. In medicine, doctors must have the knowledge to cure, but more important, they need the compassion to care. Our motivation must be to alleviate suffering without regard for material or personal gain. Yes, I knew now that there *was* more to the purpose of human existence. The question now was: Could I put that purpose into action?

SOMETHING TO CONSIDER . . .

1. From whom could you seek spiritual guidance? What would be your first question?
2. Read Matthew 25. Can you think of one meaningful way to live out Christ's words today? What can you do?
3. How could you do more to alleviate suffering in the lives of other people?

CHAPTER 3 Going Home

After that first meeting, I worked at the Tijuana shelter for a few days. I arrived around 5 a.m. to drink coffee with some of the homeless people and then assisted the sisters with patient care. Sister Sabina wanted to open a medical clinic, and I offered my advice and help toward that goal, which we ultimately achieved. In the evenings, I stayed with several Missionaries of Charity coworkers, lay people who worked with the sisters.

Mother Teresa had already been recuperating physically and spiritually at Beato Juan Diego for three weeks by the time I had arrived. She seemed extremely weak, but extremely powerful in love, compassion, and faith. Each day, I had opportunities to speak with her, and I found myself—ever the cardiologist—inquiring about how she was feeling. The answer was always the same, "There is no time to talk about it; there is too much work to be done." Then, she would walk away to feed an ill man or bathe a dying woman's face. The sisters told me that Mother Teresa had been spending much more time than usual in meditation and prayer. I concluded that she was drawing much-needed physical strength from those spiritual measures.

During my stay, I approached Sister Sabina and told her that I wished to become a coworker like those at the mission.

I asked Sister Sabina for a simple definition of what it meant to be a coworker.

"A coworker is a person who puts his or her love for God into living action and service for the poor," she replied. Again, I felt the impact of Mother's message of the purpose of life.

I had gone to Tijuana to obtain wisdom from Mother Teresa. She answered my questions, and at this point, I thought I had achieved my goal. I had acquired knowledge about my true purpose in life from a living saint. I now saw that I should always act to alleviate suffering, keeping in mind that fulfilling that purpose would determine how God would judge me at the moment of my death.

I was so content to gain this wisdom that I believed I now had everything necessary to transform my life. I realized that this would require my initiative to restructure my life. Now that I had this knowledge, I felt I was ready to go home and begin acting on what Mother Teresa had told me. Before I left, she gave me her rosary, something Sister Sabina said she had never seen Mother Teresa do for a new acquaintance.

I went back to my world. I would love to say that my transformation occurred quickly and completely, but personal growth is a slow process in which setbacks can occur almost every day. At the time, I was not mature enough, wise enough, or experienced enough to understand that simply knowing the purpose of life did not mean my transformation would take place automatically. That would require effort on my part. I also failed to ask one key question: Where did Mother Teresa's sustainable inner peace and happiness come from? When I returned home from Tijuana, I had naively convinced myself that Mother Teresa had told me all I needed to know. It was only after I began transforming my life that I recognized that something was still missing. Even though I understood my purpose, I still had not acquired the remedy or the prescription for achieving sustainable inner peace and happiness. I had not yet discerned all of Mother Teresa's prescription.

I did have some strategies in place by the time I stepped off the plane. The first was to tell my wife and daughter that I wanted to scuttle the plans for our mansion and continue to live in our modest ranch house. The only change that we would make would be to build an addition where my parents would live. My family accepted this plan more readily than one would expect. Perhaps that's because I was the materialistic aggressor. I was the one who needed the power, the control, and the possessions to justify my life and to identify myself as a success in the community.

The needs of my family members were simpler. My mother was a homemaker and my father was a public school administrator. Their financial resources had been limited throughout their lives. My wife was one of seven children of an Ohio farmer and had grown up with few material possessions—mostly hand-me-downs from older siblings. All of them simply enjoyed possessing only what they could afford or needed.

My family did notice, though, when I began giving away large sums of money to medical clinics in Mexico and to other national and international organizations serving the poor. They were worried, but they accepted my increased philanthropic efforts without complaint. Perhaps it was because they were also witnessing a transformation in me. As the amount of time and money that I was committing to the poor increased, I was becoming a more loving and self-giving person in my personal life.

Next, I turned to reordering my professional life. I had to restructure my mindset toward my patients to focus first and solely on alleviating their suffering, not on gaining power, position, titles, and control for myself. Consequently, my conversations with my family and my colleagues about the practice of medicine changed significantly. I soon learned that my path to transformation would not be free of obstacles.

SOMETHING TO CONSIDER . . .

1. What changes would you have to make in your life if you embraced Mother Teresa's prescription? Would you have to give up something, change vacation plans, or make a different career choice?
2. How would you explain those changes to your family? How might they react? How would you handle that reaction?

CHAPTER 4 The Transformation Begins: Clothing the Poor

We often fear that unless we focus on power and control as our top priority, we will jeopardize our chances to succeed as a parent, spouse, or professional. After returning from Tijuana, however, I decided that the only thing jeopardizing my career was my old attitude. I had not understood God's purpose for my life or my work as a physician. I began to take some initial and sometimes difficult steps toward change.

My first effort to put my newly found purpose to work involved finding a way to provide clothes to the poor. I contacted a local food distributor who had national connections and large semi-trucks. I hired one of his trucks and a driver. With help from several second-hand clothing stores and religious organizations that support the poor, I gathered about 80,000 pounds of clothing for Mother Teresa's mission in Tijuana. Volunteers boxed up the clothing, and the driver drove the load from Youngstown, Ohio, to San Diego and then to the U.S.–Mexico border.

So far, so good. I had flown to San Diego the day before the truck arrived and notified the sisters that the clothing was on its way. When we met at the border, however, we received bad news. Customs regulations prohibited taking the free clothing into Mexico. But with the sisters' help and the assistance of local politicians who had met Mother Teresa while she was in

Tijuana, the customs agents allowed the truck, with all its cargo intact, to travel to the Missionaries of Charity compound. The following day, volunteers unloaded the truck and distributed the clothing, mainly to the homeless men and women at the shelter.

Local lawmakers and security staff on the Mexican side of the border told me that they would never again bend the rules and allow our trucks through. That meant that we would have to find another recipient for our ever-growing clothing outreach. So many second-hand stores, local schools, and charitable organizations had pitched in that within two months after our Tijuana shipment, we had another forty tons of clothing and nowhere to send it. I contacted the Missionaries of Charity in New York City. The sisters there told me that their closest mission to Ohio was in Jenkins, Kentucky, in Appalachia.

I called Sister Judy, the superior in Jenkins, and arranged a weekend visit. School personnel in Jenkins told me that the town had an old, abandoned school that would be a perfect spot to store the clothing. So, the following month an 18-wheeler arrived in Jenkins, and volunteers helped unload and store the clothing. Again, we had a setback. The school proved too run-down to keep the clothing safe from water damage or vandalism.

Meanwhile, the calls and offers of help from representatives of second-hand stores, schools, and charitable and religious organizations kept coming. I hesitated to turn them down for fear that the program would die. Instead, I rented some storage lockers in my hometown and found alternative storage sites in Kentucky. The trucks initially left once every three months. In the first six years, the program grew enormously. Each month, a truck with about 40,000 pounds of clothing left, carrying these needed clothes to the poor. Volunteers in Appalachia now drive the trucks up to Youngstown and stay overnight. They load early in the morning under supervision from me and my

Finding a new way to clothe the poor, Dr. Wright launched a program to collect and distribute donated clothing. This United States Air Force C130 is being loaded with clothing and medical supplies for the poor in Calcutta, India.

father. We have also sent trucks loaded with clothing to Native American reservations in New Mexico, Arizona, and Utah.

The clothing project's success inspired another idea. I had heard of a peacetime program called the Denton Plan that allowed military personnel to engage in humanitarian relief work. For example, cargo planes might be used to transport medical supplies or, as I surmised, clothing to needy people throughout the world. In return, military personnel got practice stowing cargo and pilots logged flight hours. The year 1994 was a time of peace for the United States. One day, I went to the Youngstown airport, which also serves as a base for U.S. military C-5 and C-30 cargo planes, to ask officials there if loading and delivering huge boxes of clothing for the poor was something they could help me accomplish.

The colonel of the local Air Force unit told me his squadron had to go to Thailand. Rather than going west to San Francisco and then to Thailand, I asked if he could fly to the Middle East to refuel and then touch down in India before continuing to Thailand. He agreed and got permission from his superiors.

I contacted Mother Teresa and told her to expect three plane-loads full of clothing and medical aid in Calcutta. There were still hurdles to surmount. The U.S. Air Force had not flown in Indian air space for more than forty-five years. We needed military and government permission. Again, as in Mexico, Mother Teresa's influence prevailed and the planes landed in Calcutta where Sister Priscilla and other sisters from the motherhouse met them. The pilots reported that everything had gone well and that they enjoyed meeting the sisters.

Several days later, however, I received a surprise—a phone call from Mother Teresa herself. My parents, wife, and daughter were so excited to discover that she was calling that they got on portable extension phones to listen in. They heard her blessings and then listened as she said she had a serious problem to discuss. Of the boxes listed on the cargo manifest, 237 were missing. Mother Teresa was afraid someone had stolen the boxes. To her, stealing from the poor was the same as stealing from Jesus. After three days of intense searching, Air Force officials found the boxes at the airport in Youngstown. They had never even been loaded onto the planes. No one had stolen from Jesus. For me, the incident was a valuable insight into Mother Teresa's total commitment to serve the poor.

SOMETHING TO CONSIDER . . .

1. What is your primary motivation, your purpose in life? Does it reflect Mother Teresa's prescription for happiness and inner peace?
2. How could you change your primary motivation at home and at work to one of alleviating the suffering of others?
3. How much time do you have to help others? How could you find more time?

CHAPTER 5 Helping the Sick

As I continued transforming my life, I found myself involved in another project that more closely involved my work as a physician.

Several years earlier, I had become a full partner in the Ohio Heart Institute, a private cardiovascular medical center with two regional offices. The institute's success had made me extremely wealthy. Now, I found myself reexamining my power, prestige, and financial advantages. I also looked at my record of compassion. Yes, I had never denied care to anyone, even those who could not pay. But my time with Mother Teresa forced me to ask myself if those sporadic acts of charity were enough. Did they meet the standard Jesus sets for us in Matthew 25?

I thought of a way to make a more lasting difference. St. Joseph Hospital in Warren, Ohio, was closing a residency program. I asked the hospital board to revamp the program to serve the poor through a free clinic. That way, residents would get experience, and the poor and underserved would receive health care. The hospital officials saw this proposal as an extension of their stated mission: "To extend the hand of Jesus Christ to all the community, especially the marginalized and the poor." I spent a year completing this project and organized a network of 110 local physicians who were willing to accept patients in their private practice in case of an overflow from the clinic.

For my next project, I approached the executive committees of two Catholic hospitals in the area. I asked them to create an agency to help indigent people receive free medications available from pharmaceutical companies. My practice serves patients in Youngstown and Warren, Ohio, cities in the heart of what has been called America's "Rust Belt." Several economic assessments have ranked Youngstown as one of the poorest cities in Ohio, and Warren is not far behind. Obviously, the poor in those cities would benefit from a free medication program.

Free drugs are available to the poor, but physicians must fill out the forms for the patient. The process is complex and time-consuming. Not surprisingly, few doctors are willing to take the time to complete the forms and, in some cases, to tell patients that such a program even exists. Because others accept only patients with health insurance, they consider the program unnecessary. My goal was to streamline the process by creating a central agency. Physicians could refer their patients to the agency where secretaries could complete the forms.

My idea called for using some of the staff dues that physicians pay each year to their hospitals. One of the hospitals I approached had about $80,000 on hand. The foundation and administration of the hospital were receptive to the idea because it would support their mission to serve the community. I found opposition, however, from the medical staff. I asked the hospital's executive committee of physicians to add $10,000 to the funding we had already received from county commissioners and the hospital foundation. We could use the seed money from the doctors to hire secretaries to complete the burdensome paperwork. Some of the panel members balked at the idea. Several doctors wanted to invest the money in the stock market or treasury bonds. Others wanted to set it aside for special events, such as holiday parties. Another said that the task I proposed was not the medical staff's responsibility. Finally, the committee voted to table the issue. The next month, I received a note congratulating me for thinking of such

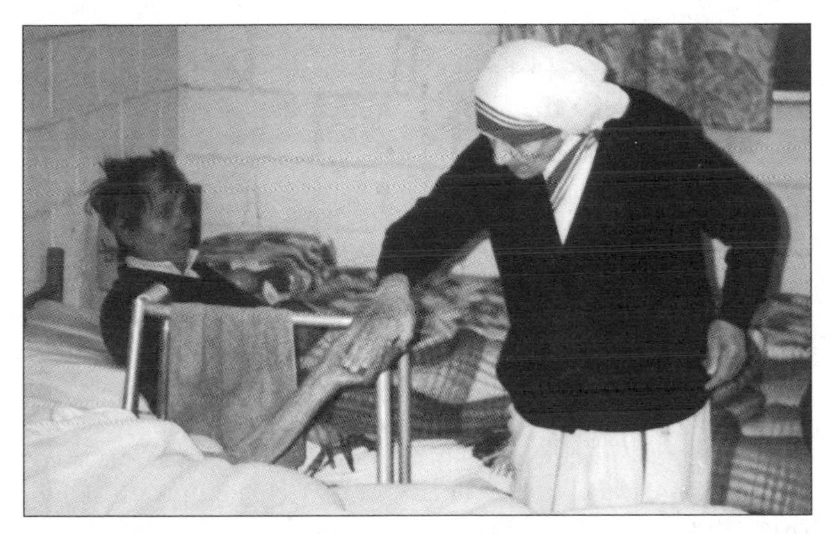

At the center for the homeless she founded in Tijuana, Mother Teresa visits and prays with homeless patients. Helping the sick and those in need, she said, will bring deep happiness and joy when the help is given out of love.

a worthy program even though the physicians in leadership could not allocate any funding for it.

At the second hospital, the proposal never even made it to a vote, even though I lobbied my case extensively with physicians. The physicians on the executive committee declared that the program was the responsibility of hospital administrators.

I had an easier time convincing the county commissioners, the hospital administration, and private foundations to allocate money for the program. Now, patients at St. Joseph Health Center in Trumbull County who cannot afford medications get two months' worth of drugs free from the hospital pharmacy. The hospital foundation buys the two-month supply which gives the program's secretaries time to enroll the patients in the free medication program. The Trumbull County program was so successful that we started another for people in nearby Mahoning County. It is supported by ten social organizations, county commissioners, bishops, and Catholic Charities. As of

January 2005, the program staff in Mahoning and Trumbull counties had each completed forms for millions of dollars worth of medications for the poor through what is now called the Medication Assistance Program.

I had made a good start, but my fellow doctors' resistance had hurt me profoundly. Mother Teresa had inspired me to do more to alleviate the suffering of others. I had offered my colleagues a way to do just that, by sharing some of what we had to help the poor, without radically altering our medical "society." They had turned me down. I had followed Mother's advice and returned home, sure that I could do work that was more meaningful now that I had discerned my purpose in life. I found myself saddened and overwhelmed, almost defeated, by forces that did not understand this true purpose of life. Even more painful was the fact that they were the same forces I had embraced and nurtured as part of the medical profession. I needed to reassess my role in life, and that led me back to Mother Teresa.

SOMETHING TO CONSIDER . . .

1. Are there areas in your life—at work, at church, or in volunteer organizations—where you could do more to alleviate suffering? How could you accomplish that?
2. How would you handle negative reactions from coworkers as you refocus your purpose of life?
3. Where would you turn for support?

CHAPTER 6 "Come, See the Work"

My second encounter with Mother Teresa came during our phone conversation about the boxes missing from the cargo planes that had flown to Calcutta. I took a moment to tell her that the knowledge she had given me about the purpose of life had motivated me to do more. But I also said that I wanted to find my own sustainable happiness and inner peace.

"If you want the answers to that question, you must come, see the work," she had replied.

Mother Teresa invited me to Calcutta. I accepted her invitation and began my years of journeying to ask Mother Teresa questions, hear her answers, and observe how she worked. In our first meeting, she helped me understand that there are many forms of hunger, thirst, and illness. I had not appeared to be hungry, thirsty, or sick, but Mother Teresa had recognized my illness and treated me. She helped me discover that alleviating the suffering of others had to be my first priority. That motivation had led me to start the clothing and medicine missions. Now I needed to seek her out again.

I had no specific questions in mind, but during that experience in Calcutta and subsequent encounters, I recognized a great number of the attitudes of spirit that defined Mother Teresa's life and work. I had the opportunity to observe her in many circumstances, conditions, and situations. I saw her responding to daily problems and events, and I recognized that she possessed powerful spiritual resources that gave her a great sense of inner peace and happiness. I refer to these as the prescription.

"Come and see the work." It made perfect sense. Doctors frequently must travel hundreds or even thousands of miles to attend conferences where experts share their knowledge on new techniques, procedures, or medications. The same desire to hear and learn from the experts is true in every profession. I find it interesting, then, that we spend so little time studying the purpose of life and finding that inner happiness that we all desire. Some of my closest friends, colleagues, and relatives thought it strange that I spent so much time traveling so many miles to work with and talk with Mother Teresa. For me, it seemed the natural thing to do.

To find Mother Teresa this second time, I went to Calcutta. It became clear to me that her inner peace and happiness did not depend on external acquisitions, but how she personally responded to circumstances and situations. She possessed an extraordinary amount of each of these spiritual attitudes. Acquiring, maintaining, and growing in these attitudes is the way to personal happiness and inner peace. It is not necessarily dependent on what happens, but on how you respond to the circumstances that life presents you.

One day, I faced that type of test on how I would respond. The sisters and I went to one of the order's clinics for people suffering from leprosy. One of the patients asked me a question:

"Why has God put me here and not you?"

I had no answer.

That same day, later in the afternoon, the man pulling my rickshaw down the street asked me the same question.

"Why has God put me here and not you?"

Again, I had no answer.

I still do not know why God puts us in various circumstances and situations. I have come to believe that God asks us to serve humanity in whatever way possible and to do it with compassion. The man pulling the rickshaw had a small, white, metal bell that he shook whenever he came up behind a horse or another animal. He exchanged his bell with me for a few rupees. Now, I keep that bell on the turn-signal arm of my car. It reminds me that God did not put me in that man's place and did not ask me to become a human horse. But God did call me to be a physician. That is the way that I serve humanity.

On that day, I had no response for the sick man or the rickshaw driver: "Why has God put me here and not you?" Mother Teresa and the loneliest person in the world helped me finally to answer that question.

SOMETHING TO CONSIDER . . .

1. Think of situations you have seen in your daily life in which you could ask: "Why has God put that person there and not me?"
2. How would you respond?

CHAPTER 7 The House of the Dying

Mother Teresa took me to the House of the Dying, the place where the sisters or government officials bring the sick, homeless, starving, and dying people found on the streets. She showed me how the coworkers of the Missionaries of Charity give love and compassion to those who are dying so that they will not feel alone, uncared for, or unloved in their last moments on earth.

When I arrived at the House of the Dying, Mother Teresa told me, "We cannot cure them. We ease their pain, give them compassion and lots of love." Just glancing at the room told me that this was a place where people came to die. I could also see that they did not die alone or unloved.

"One of the worst forms of nakedness is the lack of human dignity. The worst hunger is to be unloved, wanting love and to be nobody to anyone," Mother Teresa said.

As I walked into the room, I noticed that the workers placed the men on cots on the left side of the building and the women on the right. They were lying on mattresses that were little more than pads; their bodies were covered with sheets that were almost transparent. These were extremely skinny, underdeveloped adults suffering from infection, disease, and starvation.

The House of the Dying abuts a temple dedicated to the goddess Kali. There was a great deal of noise outside the building, where vendors were selling flowers to people who wished to honor Kali. Inside the House of the Dying, all was tranquility. Occasionally, the sound of a car horn would break through the stone walls, or a patient in pain would cry out, bringing a sister or a coworker to comfort the dying person. There was no electricity and only natural light came through the windows. On this day, the sun lit up the rooms and the patients.

Just as strong was the sense of orderliness and organization. Sisters wearing aprons gave instructions to coworkers, often wordlessly with simple nods or hand gestures. Each worker had a specific job. It reminded me of a well-run hospital where the nursing supervisors and staff focus on respecting and caring for their patients. The sisters and coworkers concentrated on bathing, feeding, talking, or praying with the sick. They were always close to their patients, frequently touching them.

Down the corridor was a room where the dead lay wrapped in sheets, awaiting either burial or cremation, according to their religion. Although this was a place of death, I did not feel a sense of sorrow. What I felt most strongly was the tranquility and peace of the House of the Dying and the compassion of people working there to alleviate the suffering of the poorest of the poor. I felt drawn to their work. This was something I could do, I thought. But God had a different job for me.

SOMETHING TO CONSIDER . . .

1. Is there a type of work you have always longed to do? What kept you from following that goal?
2. How would you incorporate that work into your life? What changes would it require?
3. How would performing this work show compassion and alleviate the suffering of others?

CHAPTER 8 Learning to Serve

I stood with Mother Teresa, asking her questions about where the people had come from and who brought them to the House of the Dying. I wondered what medical care and professional assistance she could offer them. She did not have time to answer any of my questions because a small ambulance arrived and the porters brought a human being into the House of the Dying. I say "human being" because I could not tell if the person on the stretcher was a man or a woman, even though the patient was alert and responsive. I could tell immediately that the patient was dying from gangrene that was destroying both legs and the right arm. Maggots were eating away at the patient's rotting limbs.

The smell was unbearable.

Mother directed the volunteers to place the patient on a bed. Then she asked me to put on a cloth apron and gloves and help her remove the patient's clothing so that we could bathe the gangrenous limbs with warm water. Suddenly, I was responsible for providing one-on-one care to someone who assuredly had no more than two hours of life left.

As a doctor, I have seen people mangled and bloodied by car accidents, train wrecks, gunshots, and stabbings. Never have I seen anyone in such a desperate condition as the person Mother Teresa was asking me to help. I could not simply check the patient's vital signs, write a few orders on a chart, and then turn the case over to a nurse or resident. I did not have morphine or Demerol to dull the dying person's agony. I did not have antibiotics or intravenous fluids to administer. I did not have surgeons or infectious disease experts to consult.

The only thing I had was my hands.

In my world, it is common for doctors to use high-tech medical equipment to help a patient, but it is unheard of for a doctor to stay with a patient for two hours simply to bathe his wounds and let him know that someone loves him. The unfamiliarity of this situation gave me a sudden and enormous sense of being alone, incompetent, and deficient. Then, as I helped remove the patient's clothing, the dying person's suffering and loneliness overwhelmed me. I recoiled from the stench of the infected wounds and tissue and walked out of the House of the Dying.

I sat on the steps and watched the Hindu priests and the Hindu faithful in procession by the thousands. They were taking turns worshiping Kali. For twenty minutes I watched, and then Mother Teresa and one of the sisters came outside and sat beside me.

I could not stop apologizing to Mother Teresa. I told her how incompetent, ashamed, and embarrassed I felt because I could not carry out the simple task of bathing a dying patient.

"Nor could I if I did not think that I was bathing and treating Jesus Christ in the distressing disguise of the poor," she said.

Then she smiled. Once again, her words gave me a new perspective on my life.

"Dr. Paul, I do things that you cannot do, and you do things that I cannot do, but together, we can do beautiful things for God." We never discussed this experience again.

Mother Teresa restored my self-respect by showing me how to answer the question that both the leper and the rickshaw driver had asked: God places each one of us in conditions and circumstances that are unique. We are all required and expected to serve, but how we serve is a decision that we make with

Missionaries of Charity enter the leprosy colony they run in Calcutta, India. When Dr. Wright served there, he helped provide thousands of pairs of rubber flip-flop sandals for lepers who are often injured when they lose sensation in their feet and unknowingly step on sharp objects.

God's help. It involves only God and us as individuals. I should have given that answer to the leper and the rickshaw driver. God calls all of us to serve, but our unique talents, abilities, and situations mean that we cannot all serve in the same way. God does not put us all in the same place. We must assess our God-given talents and use them to serve others with compassion to alleviate their suffering. What capacity, what profession, where and how we do this is a decision we as individuals reach with God. The important point is that to do God's work, we must serve others.

Mother Teresa asked me to go back into the House of the Dying and feed some of the people who were able to eat and drink. The sisters gave me a mixture that appeared to be puffed rice and banana moistened with water. It was a simple and nourishing concoction, yet something the sick and suffering could digest easily. I spent the rest of the day sitting and feeding the people of the House of the Dying. Completing this humble task gave me the beautiful feeling that I was truly doing God's work. Now, every morning before going to the hospital, I eat a small cup of puffed wheat or puffed rice with a bit of banana to remind me of Mother's lesson that day.

I knew that my calling was different from those who felt at home in the House of the Dying. I asked Mother Teresa where I could best serve others. Again, her advice was a revelation. "You must go home and grow in love and compassion in your own community," she said. "The streets of Calcutta lead to everyone's door." Mother Teresa knew that it is much easier to get on an airplane and fly to a foreign country to serve the poor than it is to go home and serve the poor daily within your own community. Home was where I was needed.

SOMETHING TO CONSIDER . . .

1. How has God called you to serve in a unique way? Think of your job, volunteer activities, people you encounter every day.
2. What are the needs of your immediate community? How could you serve them?

CHAPTER 9 Home Again

The most important part of my journey became the one back to my home in Youngstown, Ohio. I came home with the realization that I had never seen true compassion until I was with Mother Teresa and watched her work in the House of the Dying in Calcutta. From that experience of perfect compassion and by working with her and her order in other places around the world, I discovered my purpose in life. In turn, I found the prescription that changed my life.

Now that I was home again, the time had come to ask myself, "Who am I?"

On a superficial level, I could respond that I was Paul A. Wright, M.D., cardiologist. Because I had held that title for so many years, that answer had become my instinctive response. I could also have added that I was a husband and father. I could tell people about my family background, what I do during the day, the number of patients I see, the types of procedures I perform. The bottom line was that none of those things really explained my value system and my thoughts.

Why had I become a doctor? Was it to help others, or was I consciously or subconsciously seeking the power, prestige, and wealth that this career often brings? Is that why I still had not found the inner peace and happiness that Mother Teresa seemed to embody? What was her secret?

I tried to think as Mother Teresa would and tried to apply her message from the Gospel of Matthew to my life as a physician. This thought finally occurred to me: In our Western culture of materialism and competition, the primary purpose for us in life—whether we're willing to acknowledge it or not—is a self-serving one. We tend to put material gain or expediency, not service, first. That mindset reduces work to a mere business, whether you are a doctor, stockbroker, teacher, or a stay-at-home parent.

So who am I? Who are you? To know another well, you have to know the person's character. You must have knowledge of how the person responds to circumstances and his or her motivation. You need to know that person's philosophy or prescription for life. Most people do not have one. Or if they do, they cannot articulate it. But that prescription is who you are and how others will truly know us. As a man thinks, so he is; as a man continues to think, so shall he remain.

I still practice medicine at the Ohio Heart Institute with many of the same partners I had in 1992. Even though I still work long hours, I see fewer patients than I did then. With the help of Mother's inspiration, I have been able to cure myself of a certain mindset. I once thought that materialism is the only acceptable way of life, that exhaustion is the consequence of such a lifestyle, and that ever-present feelings of desperation and dissatisfaction are the norm. Instead, I have a new relationship with God and with others. I have a new awareness that self-sacrifice to serve God and humanity is the essence of life's purpose. The only investment that I am called to make is to invest my humanity in serving others. Am I a one hundred percent, round-the-clock happy person? No, but I can say that most of my days are filled with enjoyment and pleasure that I gain by serving my patients for the correct reason.

My first contact with Mother Teresa spurred me to start charitable activities at home. The shipment of clothing that we collected for India led me to experience Mother Teresa at work in her true home in Calcutta. Now I see that all this was part of a journey. My travels had taken me from Youngstown to Mexico and India to see Mother Teresa. Later, I journeyed to her missions in places like Kentucky, to her soup kitchens and homeless shelters in Harlem and the Bronx, to her AIDS house in Washington, D.C. Finally, after her death in 1997, I went to St. Peter's Square in the Vatican.

On Sunday, October 19, 2003, I joined hundreds of thousands of others in St. Peter's Square in the Vatican to witness the beatification of Mother Teresa by Pope John Paul II. The woman who was called a living saint by so many during her lifetime was now moving much closer to canonization as a saint in the Catholic church. As I listened to the pope's homily, I heard the distillation of everything I had seen and experienced in my contact with Mother Teresa and her work. Pope John Paul II spoke of her self-sacrifice, service to the poor, humility, compassion, and purpose of life. He called upon heaven to "help us be gentle and humble of heart, like this fearless messenger of love. Help us serve every person we meet with joy and a smile." I again saw how all these elements he singled out fit together to form a prescription for happiness and inner peace.

SOMETHING TO CONSIDER . . .

1. What are you like as a person? What qualities define your character? What qualities do you strive for that you feel you lack?
2. How do you think others see you? What word would most people use to describe your character?

CHAPTER 10 The Purpose of Life and Mother Teresa's Prescription

The key to changing my life was to adopt an attitude of compassion that went beyond the desire to simply alleviate suffering. That was the purpose of life I had learned from Mother Teresa's teaching and work. To sustain my motivation toward this purpose of life, I knew I needed once again to tap into Mother Teresa's knowledge. I needed to find the elements that would sustain me. I thought about the qualities that sustained Mother Teresa and her Missionaries of Charity as they went about serving the poorest of the poor and started to list them. From this exercise, the prescription evolved.

Just what is this prescription? I discovered that it consists of ten attitudes of spirit: commitment to community, reverence for all human life, compassion and love, contentment and gratitude, faith, humility, tolerance, patience, forgiveness, and honesty. Each one grows out of the way in which Mother Teresa conducted her daily life and relationships.

I would like to share examples of each component of the prescription and thoughts to consider on how we can incorporate these ten attitudes into our lives. Be aware that we must nurture all the attitudes of the prescription.

You must understand that happiness and sustainable peace depend on maintaining and continuing to take this prescription. My healing had nothing to do with external acquisitions; it was internal, mental, spiritual healing. Mother Teresa gave me the prescription, but I was responsible for using it and healing myself. No one else could do it for me. I had to accept this new way of life. Once I was committed to maintaining and sustaining the prescription, I began feeling at peace with God, humanity, and myself.

An intense aspiration to follow the prescription has a very strong impact on others. What a wonderful thing we would achieve if we could teach our children from a young age to cultivate a proper value system. We could offer them a prescription or formula that would allow them to achieve happiness and inner peace while serving others rather than simply serving themselves and their self-interest.

If you feel something is missing in your work or life, and if you are looking for something outside yourself, you will not find it. Whatever's missing must take root inside you. It cannot be found by acquiring more material possessions or a job promotion. It cannot be found by sheltering yourself on a warm, secluded beach or in another seemingly stress-free environment. You will know that you have succeeded when you are surrounded by the storm and confusion of life, yet feel serene and confident. You must discern how God calls you to serve in the community. Then, take the steps needed to fulfill that purpose of life.

Mother Teresa's prescription can be applied to people of all faiths. She never based a decision to serve—or not to serve—anyone on the person's religion. The person's urgent need for help and comfort was her guideline. As Mother Teresa would often say, "Nurturing and teaching a human being to become more loving and compassionate makes a Hindu a better Hindu, a Muslim a better Muslim, a Jew a better Jew, and a Buddhist a better Buddhist." This is a message of community. In other words, by following her prescription we can all become better in God's eyes and build a better relationship with others and with God.

Please take one step at a time and do not rush. Whenever I expressed a worry about whether I was doing enough or giving enough, Mother would always say, "I do not want you to worry about that. Just continue to grow in compassion and love."

You do not have to adopt the elements of the prescription in any particular order or in haste. Enjoy the journey and know that you will realize your purpose of life and experience peace and happiness in God's time.

SOMETHING TO CONSIDER . . .

1. Do you see any of these ten attitudes of spirit recommended by Mother Teresa in your life? Which ones?
   1. Commitment to community
   2. Reverence for all human life
   3. Compassion and love
   4. Contentment and gratitude
   5. Faith
   6. Humility
   7. Tolerance
   8. Patience
   9. Forgiveness
   10. Honesty
2. Which attitudes of spirit would you like to see taking root or developing in you now?

PART 2 Mother's Prescription

CHAPTER 11 Why Do I Need the Prescription?

While I was training as a cardiologist, I moonlighted in the emergency room at St. Elizabeth Health Center in Youngstown, Ohio. On every shift, the ambulances brought in a stream of people. Some had gunshot wounds, some came with stab wounds, others had heart attacks or similar life-threatening conditions. All of these patients were obviously in great pain and distress, but the ones in the worst shape got the staff's immediate attention.

This type of pain is so different from the constant suffering that we all feel emotionally, whether it's stress, fear, anxiety, or desire. Many of these mental sufferings are self-inflicted. We cannot resolve them by going to the emergency room for sutures or medication. We must seek God, and Mother Teresa's prescription to heal our own spiritual suffering.

The problem comes in recognizing that we are suffering. We have become numb to the constant state of tension, anger, and dissatisfaction. Eventually, we must recognize that we are hemorrhaging our happiness, energy, and peace of mind. Before we bleed to death spiritually, we must take action.

Take the example of the man who suffers a heart attack. He may be making a sales presentation to a room full of potential clients or playing soccer in the backyard with his children. Whatever is going on is forgotten in the rush to get the man to the hospital and save his life. Contrast that reaction with the way we handle our emotional suffering and pain, our anxieties, our dissatisfactions. Perhaps because we know that they cannot be resolved by going to the emergency room, we accept them as part of our daily routine. We must wake up to this pain; it has gone on too long and the suffering has become too severe to continue any longer. When we do this, we may be ready to take the next step—adopting Mother Teresa's prescription.

The symptoms of our illness can manifest themselves as personal greed, discontent, insensitivity, self-obsession, resentment, impatience, stress, anxiety, fear, or any other form of negative energy. You must recognize these symptoms and rush to the emergency room in your spirit. You could find help in Mother's prescription. Sometimes these symptoms recur several times a day, but over time, you will find that you have "dosed" yourself sufficiently. Now, you can sustain your inner peace and happiness.

Will this prescription affect other people? Will they be more honest, kind, or sensitive in dealing with you? The answer is probably not. But I have found enormous peace, serenity, and happiness that I am sure I would never have acquired had I not heard Mother's message and discovered her therapy for happiness.

The first purpose of Mother's message and prescription is to help you first heal yourself. By doing so, you become an example to others who witness your new perspective. Do not try early on to make close family members, friends, or relatives listen to the message or to take the prescription. They may not yet have sensed their own inner suffering. Let them observe as you grow in tolerance, humility, contentment, and all the other positive qualities that result from the prescription.

In the following chapters, we will look at each of the ten spiritual attitudes linked to the prescription and explore how you can add them to your life.

SOMETHING TO CONSIDER . . .

1. What are your pains, anxieties, and frustrations?
2. How do you deal with them now?
3. How could Mother Teresa's approach to healing help you deal with personal hurts, injuries, or stress?

CHAPTER 12 Commitment to Community

Achieving peace and happiness does not happen in a vacuum. Mother Teresa recognized that souls need to be nurtured in a certain environment. She and her sisters spent a great deal of time in meditation and prayer throughout the day. It started with Mass early in the morning and included adoration of the eucharist and evening prayers. Mother Teresa surrounded herself and her sisters with prayer and an environment that supported serving the poorest of the poor. She always focused her actions and thoughts toward self-giving and service.

Anyone trying to take Mother's advice must first take steps to protect his or her environment. For example, you would not want to socialize or spend too much time with people who are extremely materialistic. If you have addictions, the need to stay out of surroundings that promote those addictions is obvious. Finding a mentor is another help. Someone you admire may be willing to share spiritual insights with you. Seek a teacher who has the qualifications to teach what you wish to learn and emulate that person.

Mother Teresa and her sisters developed a unique and positive mindset. They spent considerable time in prayer and in an environment that focused on their work. This gave the sisters the reinforcement, energy, and positive example they needed so that they could "pray their work." Their works of compassion were prayers. What followed from those prayers was a sense of peace and happiness. You can do this as well. By keeping your actions focused on alleviating the suffering of others, your work becomes a prayer. Work does not have to stop for prayer and prayer does not have to stop for work.

Often, the ability to follow Mother's prescription is affected by circumstances within our environment. I often saw Mother Teresa protecting the spiritual environment for her sisters. How we respond to Mother's prescription will depend upon what we read, what we see on television, whom we associate with, and our work, home, or social environment. We are called to be vigilant and to recognize circumstances, people, and influences that either aid or jeopardize our ability to follow Mother's prescription and the Christian lifestyle.

Controlling my environment is simpler when I am around my patients. That is when I can concentrate on alleviating suffering. Sometimes I am with physicians or hospital administrators who seem to be too politically or materialistically motivated. Sometimes I have difficulty dealing with them. I have to resist the danger of entangling myself in their hidden agendas and becoming angry and frustrated.

Some circumstances should simply be avoided, especially those contrary to a peaceful and self-giving atmosphere. If you get involved in this kind of situation, follow Mother Teresa's guidelines. If you hold the chair or directorship of a department, for example, and administrators and other colleagues cannot appreciate or understand your perspective and the basis for your decisions, then this may not be the place for you. The best idea might be to leave that environment, that is, resign from that position. You are not obligated to remain in a place where your happiness and inner peace are jeopardized by pressure from other people. This is not a cop-out. If your focus is to alleviate the sufferings of others, the primary objective would be to develop programs and projects that will achieve that goal.

Mother Teresa poses with sisters who have just taken their final vows. Professed sisters take vows of poverty, chastity, and obedience and an additional vow to provide wholehearted and free service to the poorest of the poor. Missionaries of Charity now serve on every continent and in most countries of the world.

When faced with an environment that challenges your inner peace and happiness, keep these thoughts in mind. Understand that these people are suffering. A great deal of their suffering is self-inflicted, just as yours once was. Remind yourself whom you are really working for and whose work it is. You are working for your brothers and sisters, and this work is God's work. Knowing this will give you intensity and an enormous sense of dignity, personal accomplishment, and purpose, even in the face of resistance or ridicule.

The painful movement toward inner peace and happiness is a healing pain. It manifests itself as discomfort in an environment where people perceive you as eccentric or uninformed because you have abandoned or are unconcerned about excessive personal gain. You must be able to give up these associations and move on. Make yourself at home with those who support your goals: philanthropic programs, foundation boards, or community centers where you will be surrounded by others who are focused on service and the alleviation of suffering.

Yes, it is uncomfortable, even frightening, to face the possibility of relinquishing the familiar community or environment to which you are accustomed. Doing so brings a positive result, just as giving up those slices of Boston cream pie after every dinner will result in lost pounds. Eventually, you will see and feel the positive change. Eventually, you are happier with the result.

As a cardiologist, the best way for me to explain this is with the example of the patients who come to my office complaining of tightness in the chest and shortness of breath. I perform a heart catheterization to diagnose the source of the symptoms. When patients must undergo surgery, I explain that they will be exchanging their preoperative, ongoing pain for postsurgical pain. That pain, however, is the healing pain. It will eventually go away. Without surgery, the chest tightness and lack of breath will continue, and in many cases, get worse and lead to death.

At first, patients complain that their surgical pain is worse than what they suffered before surgery. Six weeks after the operation, however, an amazing change has occurred. Many of them openly admit that they have given up unhealthy appetites for alcohol, cigarettes, or fatty foods. They are exercising and taking medication properly. Their energy has increased and their discomfort is minimal. They have endured the healing pain and have moved on to a healthier life.

You must also fight the temptation to do the work just for the sake of the work. There is no peace and happiness in such a superficial purpose. I am not saying that you shouldn't take on more responsibility or leadership if you feel called to do so. Just be honest about why you are seeking that loftier title or position. You can do so by allowing yourself to be guided first by compassion in your decisions. Then consider what is best for the community, especially the poor and underserved.

Mother Teresa neither recognized nor accepted the criticism of those who found fault with her for avoiding involvement in international organizations. God had not called her to that work. She believed that type of involvement would distract her from her true purpose: to serve the poorest of the poor. In her eyes, she could not be all things to all people and serve in all capacities. She maintained a proper mindset and goals based on her calling to serve. The same must be true for us. We cannot do everything, and we cannot be all things to all people. God calls each of us to serve in a unique way.

Many times, it's not possible to serve while maintaining a position of prestige or leadership. In my professional life, my ego got a boost when I became the chief of a hospital's internal medicine or cardiology departments. But no matter how passionate I was about being selfless and fair, I often had to deal with colleagues who attempted to manipulate staff and administrators for their own gain. The added responsibility and conflicts left me feeling detached from my patients. Finally, I decided to resign from all leadership positions except the ones that focused on community service and patient care. Those, I discovered, were compatible with my sense of purpose, and their environment supported my goal to serve with compassion.

In my personal life, I can look to my daughter as an example of how to maintain the proper community. Maria Alana has a beautiful heart, full of light, compassion, warmth, and trust in herself and others. During her time in college, she belonged to a sorority. She told me one day that occasionally her sorority sisters argued and that their disagreements sometimes resulted in verbal aggression. Maria said she regretted not being more assertive then, even when she was the person being insulted or offended. Instead, she preferred to walk away from the argument or confrontation. Eventually, she moved out of the sorority house. I told her that what she saw as a weakness was really a strength, one that I had spent years trying to develop.

Once you have a firm understanding of your purpose in life, that is, your special vocations to serve others, you will find yourself bonded to others with the same mindset. The peace and serenity of that community will sustain you.

SOMETHING TO CONSIDER . . .

1. Mother Teresa suggested that we must have a community or environment that nurtures our spiritual growth and our vocation to serve others. How would you rate your environment or community? Very supportive? Somewhat supportive? Not at all supportive? Describe this environment.
2. Make a list of specific changes that might help build a community or environment that would support your new purpose in life.

CHAPTER 13 Reverence for Human Life

Mother Teresa believed that if governments and individuals acquired respect and reverence for human life, we could save our world from destruction. When we acquire a critical level of respect for life, we will not have to worry about atomic bombs or terrorists. We will not have to worry about conflicts of interest and diverse religious doctrines. Instead, respect for human life will be paramount and we will strive to protect it at all costs. Wars will cease, along with hunger and inadequate health care. Peace and happiness will follow.

In recent years, we have been forced to face many moral and ethical issues, including abortion, that contradict respect for life. We must recognize that disregarding the sanctity of life is often based on convenience or the profit motive even though the person making the decision insists that he or she is acting out of love or compassion. That person is devaluing human life. If a society develops laws that reduce respect for human life or degrade its dignity, then we are denying the value of life. Arguing that a human life must be terminated because someone is nonproductive, too old, defective, or just a fetus is not valid if one accepts that every life is created in God's image. By assigning qualifications for the right to human life, we place ourselves on a slippery slope. Consciously or unconsciously, we are devaluing all human life.

The fact that a human life is unborn or near death, or physically or mentally deficient, in no way diminishes the amount of pain and suffering that these brothers and sisters experience. Too often for the sake of convenience or financial profit, we marginalize these people and thus reduce our reverence and respect for humanity. We must force ourselves to be aware of this danger. We must maintain compassion and the desire to alleviate suffering at all levels of existence as our primary goal. All forms of compassion require some renouncing of self-interest. So, you must give yourself up for others. Your sacrifice, however, benefits both humanity and you. You are allowing yourself to grow in peace and happiness.

As a physician, I have been called to sit with families deciding whether to resuscitate a loved one who is gravely ill. Sometimes, the family members show more love by deciding to let the loved one go, rather than sustaining life when it means compromising that person's dignity and prolonging suffering. We must reverence the dignity of life. But as death approaches, we must also recognize that the dying person deserves dignity as he or she passes from this life.

Mother Teresa was untroubled by criticism of her uncompromising devotion to human life. Serving God "in the distressing disguise of the poor," as she put it, was her only concern. In 1994 she led the National Prayer Breakfast for the U.S. Congress. Someone asked what solutions there were for preventing a nuclear holocaust. Some officials at the breakfast suggested a moratorium on the construction of nuclear warheads or a limit on the number of nations that owned nuclear weapons. Others felt that such restrictions were unrealistic since nations would find illicit ways to obtain such weapons.

To Mother Teresa, none of these ideas had validity. She embraced a much more fundamental solution. She saw the world as a place where there is too much hurry, where parents do not have time for their children, and spouses have no time for each other. For Mother Teresa, world peace began in the

Sister Sabina, superior for the Missionaries of Charity Home for the Poor in Tijuana, sits with several local children waiting for a medical check-up in a medical van. Reverence for life, Mother Teresa taught, must include caring for the hungry, sick, and lonely.

home. The deterioration of world peace begins there as well, with intolerance, impatience, and lack of respect for those closest to us. If we cannot respect those we love, how can we respect strangers? If that respect grows in our homes, we cannot help but take it with us when we leave to do our daily work.

Mother Teresa wanted us to teach our children reverence for human life, to show them that each person is a brother or sister and a child of God. She was convinced that if we could grow into a world family, there would be no need for nuclear weapons. As always, her idea for saving and serving humanity was rooted in love, compassion, and reverence for all life.

SOMETHING TO CONSIDER . . .

1. How do you promote reverence for human life in your community, in your home?
2. How does compassion for others in your life fit in with building respect for life?

CHAPTER 14 Compassion and Love

I asked Mother Teresa the meaning of compassion, and she explained that it is the desire to alleviate the suffering of others. I asked her how much compassion I must have. She asked me not to feel guilty, but to become more concerned about the suffering of others, and to grow in my desire to alleviate their suffering. I then asked her to define holiness. She said, "Holiness is nothing more than enjoying doing God's work."

In my experience as a cardiologist, I have found that most of my colleagues are extremely well trained and knowledgeable. The question becomes, then, what is their motivation? Some doctors hope to gain referrals from the patient or the patient's primary care physician and thus enjoy financial gain. Others want to perform well to avoid the threat of a malpractice lawsuit. All these motivations are acceptable ways of doing a physician's job; however, they displace the desire to alleviate suffering as a primary motivation.

The hundreds of medical students, interns, and residents I have met over the past twenty years all tell me the same thing—it is extremely rare for professors in medical schools to discuss compassion or its role as a motivator. My only real exposure to the topic of compassion took place during the semester I studied medical ethics at the University of Notre Dame.

The compassion deficiency carries through into our hospitals and doctors offices. I completed six years of residency and fellowship at a Catholic health care facility. Never did our daily noon conferences involve a discussion of the concept of compassion. I have attended dozens of departmental, staff, and executive committee meetings. While a few of the meetings began with a prayer, we never talked about compassion—just the business of practicing medicine. We talked about ways to reduce patients' lengths of stay in the hospital, staff disciplinary issues, hospital regulations, and other issues that have a financial impact on our practice or the hospital.

Perhaps we shy away from that discussion because compassion is such a complex concept. Do not confuse compassion with pity, which demands no action or selflessness on our part. Real compassion, rather, has several different levels. The first level touches the surface. An example might be a prayer we say asking God to alleviate the suffering of others. The second level adds a component of action. We might give an hour each week to serve food at the local soup kitchen. Or we might write a check to a charity we admire. Neither of these two levels involves a great deal of sacrifice or pain, but we still derive pleasure from knowing that we are advancing God's work in a small way.

The third level of compassion involves actually giving up time or money that someone might have spent on himself or herself. It could mean sacrificing a vacation or new clothes to alleviate the suffering of others. At this level, the compassionate person sacrifices a bit. The next level of compassion involves recognizing an injustice and assuming the responsibility to resolve the problem. Some examples might be to assume the financial responsibility for a charitable program or to administer a program to serve the poor.

Mother Teresa embodied this ultimate level of compassion. She was a person who dedicated her life to alleviating the suffering of others with almost no regard for herself. The ancient Greeks referred to this type of love as *agape*. It is the term the Scriptures used to refer to God's love—total commitment of self to others, asking nothing for yourself and giving yourself completely to others.

Finding someone like Mother Teresa who possesses this type of total compassion and love is rare. Observing this human perfection inspires us to become more compassionate and loving. This is what we mean, I think, when we say someone is "fully alive." The person who embodies total compassion and love is happiest and most fulfilled in a profession or activity that focuses on alleviating the suffering of others. We must ask ourselves how often we concentrate 100 percent on the needs of someone else, rather than on what we stand to gain from our interactions with others.

I personally did not know how much of myself I was required to give. I asked Mother Teresa this specific question: "Sometimes, I feel I do not give enough of myself, my time, or my finances. How much do I give?" Her response was, "Sh." She placed her hand on mine and said, "I do not want you to worry about this. I want you to grow in compassion and love, to resolve the suffering of others. I do not want you to be preoccupied with thinking and worrying if you are giving enough or serving enough."

Then, she waved her hand in the air and said, "I am your mother. I take this worry away from you." It gave me a tremendous amount of inner peace to understand that I was not required to give some specific percentage of income or time. The only thing God required of me was that I continually challenge myself to grow in compassion and love.

Sometimes we need help recognizing how to challenge ourselves. Mother and the sisters often told the story of the wealthy Hindu woman who came to Mother Teresa asking how she could become more charitable. Mother knew that the woman was a member of a high caste and that she had certain community expectations and responsibilities to meet. Mother told her that the next time she bought a new sari she should buy one that cost 100 rupees less than she would have spent.

Then spend 100 rupees less on the next one and so on. The money she did not spend on herself should go to the poor. In this way, Mother Teresa showed the woman how to become more selfless and self-sacrificing, and how to begin in herself a revolution of not only charity, but also compassion and love.

Mother Teresa helped me apply this concept to my life. She liked to tell people, "The streets of Calcutta lead to everyone's door." So when I asked her when I should return to Calcutta, she advised me not to. She suggested that I use the money I would have spent on plane fare to begin programs or projects in my community. Mother recognized that it would be easy to go to a faraway place for a short time, help people there, and then return to a normal, self-centered life. She knew that it was more difficult to love and be patient, tolerant, and compassionate with those in our own communities every day of our lives.

God will judge us this way: "I was hungry and you fed me, I was naked and you clothed me, I was thirsty and you gave me drink, I was sick and you tended to me." Jesus' meaning is clear: we must grow in love and compassion. The first question we must ask is, what is our primary motivation? Is it to serve others? No work, no matter how well done, has value in God's eyes unless it satisfies this requirement. Our work should be motivated to resolve suffering by serving humanity.

During one of the celebrations of final vows for new sisters of the Missionaries of Charity, I asked Mother Teresa how she decided where to serve or how to serve. Her response was, "I'm not concerned about the religious beliefs of those I serve but focus only on the urgency of the need. If there is any preference among the people we serve, it is for the poorest of the poor, the most abandoned, the most lonely, the sickest, the most hungry, and the lepers."

The very fact that God has placed a certain person in your path is a sign that God wants you to do something for that person. Such encounters do not occur by chance. We are

Mother Teresa gives some plastic rosaries to one of the patients at the medical clinic she established in Tijuana, Mexico. "Let anyone who comes to you go away feeling better and happier," she said, describing her approach to serving with compassion.

bound to serve God's will by opening ourselves to compassion and love. In this way, we alleviate that person's suffering.

We must also realize that the only way we can truly serve in a selfless manner with no consideration of self is to serve the poorest of the poor, those who cannot reciprocate in any way. This change in mindset is what moves us from practicing the mere business of our profession to humanitarianism.

Your service could be as simple as Mother Teresa's admonition to "let anyone who comes to you go away feeling better and happier." However humble the service to another, when the primary motivation behind the act is compassion, it is of great value in God's eyes. This also produces a closer connection to God. If you wish to find peace and happiness, grow in compassion and love for others, especially the poor.

Often, we are discouraged by circumstances that seem beyond our control, for example, the problem of starvation throughout the world. Compassion could alleviate this problem! God has given us adequate resources to feed every person in the world, but we simply do not care enough or love others enough to institute the appropriate international measures to distribute those resources. Such an effort would be a great work of peace, as all works of compassion are. Even great compassion, however, does not free you from the obligation to be knowledgeable in your profession. You must be competent. It is not enough just to act, you must act well.

One final thought: Mother Teresa told me that no matter how well we do our work, if there is no love or compassion motivating the work, the effort has no value in God's eyes. The presence of love and compassion is what gives value to the work. She told me, "Our life has no meaning and no other motivation other than caring for him, feeding him, clothing him, visiting him, in the distressing disguise of the poor."

SOMETHING TO CONSIDER . . .

1. Consider the wealthy woman and her saris. How can you incorporate more compassion into your life through small steps?
2. How is your present work motivated by compassion and love? Are there ways that this can grow?

CHAPTER 15 Contentment and Gratitude

Mother Teresa was not one to sit around conference tables for long hours, discussing issues and strategies. Her focus was on one person at a time, serving that individual's need and serving God through that person. Right now, people are hungry, need medical care, or require comfort. Her purpose in life was to fulfill an immediate need as quickly as she could, and that made her content. By doing this, she and the poor people she served inspired others to carry out works of compassion and love.

The first step toward acquiring contentment is finding a purpose in life. By embracing and understanding Mother's message, you realize that you are called to serve others and alleviate their suffering. Knowing that purpose and struggling to obtain a mindset to grow in that purpose gave me an enormous sense of contentment. I knew that I was an important part of a plan that was much bigger than I. Being part of God's plan and doing his will took the place of striving for more possessions or recognition.

Being content with what we have is difficult because our society does not recognize the desire for excessive material possessions as an addiction. We acknowledge substance addictions that destroy our happiness and health and threaten our relationships with others. Yet, there are other addictions that are not inhaled, injected, or consumed. These are addictions to greed, egoism, pride, impatience, intolerance, and holding grudges. Unlike drug or alcohol addictions, our society does not see them as health-threatening conditions. Indeed, some addictions, such as the addiction to materialism, are often applauded and encouraged as signs of success and happiness. Feeding an addiction—such as buying that new outfit—brings the same momentary surge of pleasure that having another drink gives an alcoholic. The ultimate consequence, however, is frustration. The desire for more things reminds us of the drug addict who craves another, stronger, but ultimately more entrapping, "fix."

We must give up these addictions and become content with what we have if we want to achieve spiritual healing. For example, Mother Teresa would say that money is not evil in itself. Excessive desire for money and the things it can buy is extremely damaging to the soul. Money in itself can do great work, but love of money for the sake of acquiring money is self-destructive. Mother Teresa often pointed out that the desire for money led Judas to betray Jesus.

The more you need, the less chance there is that you will be happy with yourself. We take out enormous mortgages, max out five or six credit cards, or use our savings to pay for extravagant vacations. Some of us feel the daily stress of wondering how we will answer the calls from debt collectors. Indeed, a million people in the United States go bankrupt each year. We cannot trust God to bail us out of every financial difficulty. Doing God's work means recognizing that we cannot satisfy every material desire we have.

By following Mother Teresa's prescription, you can find happiness. To alter our sense of well-being, we must come to grips with worthy human values and grow in these values. At the same time we must learn to recognize the existence of negative values, including the excessive desire for material wealth.

In the year 2000, one of my partners started an investment club in which physicians shared their "knowledge" of various stocks, especially high-tech and dot-com offerings. I attended one of these meetings and was impressed by the sophisticated financial discussion. Now, many of my colleagues are depressed over the money they lost on these boom stocks. Many of them concluded that their stock purchases amounted to little more than gambling. Had they recognized then that excessive greed was hindering their ability to make a rational decision, they would not have lost so much later.

In our country, we find discontent in a multitude of ways. We focus on whether we are tall enough, thin enough, fashionable enough. We are unhappy with the weather, the size of our house, the make of our car, the lack of a promotion in our job. We surround ourselves with discontent and dissatisfaction because we believe that having something different or better will make our life better. Contentment, however, does not mean giving up a desire for more or a desire for something different. It simply means that today I will be happy with what happens to me. I will be content with my life, knowing that I am doing the best that I can, and that what follows is God's will. As Mother Teresa so often said, "God does not make mistakes." By directing my life to its proper purpose and disciplining my mind to Mother's prescription for living, I can be content. I know that the consequences are as they should be since they are God's will. I can be content knowing that I thought, spoke, and acted well.

If we spend our days worrying about how we will pay the mortgage or whether we will lose the things we possess, we have little time left to serve others. Contentment comes from the inner sense of knowing that you are focused on doing God's work. The consequences of your actions are in His hands. This is a freer way of living.

Similarly, if you choose a profession because it promises great material rewards, but are doing work that is tedious or unsuited to your real calling, then you are destined to be dissatisfied. On the other hand, if you are truly in the right profession, yet desire more than that profession could ever offer, you are also destined for discontent. Determining which profession or role best suits us can take years. You may be wired to be a chef, but not to run your own restaurant. Finding your place in life happens by taking on responsibilities that suit you and discarding ones that do not. Those that drive you toward goals of power and control rather than toward the service of others will not make you happy.

Instead of judging ourselves on how much money we make, we should judge ourselves on our ability to maintain and follow the advice from Mother Teresa. Any thought, word, or action not compatible with the prescription has the potential to damage us and make us discontented. Many times a lifestyle that contradicts Mother Teresa's prescription appears to be worthwhile. It can energize you for a short time. Ultimately, however, acting in opposition to the prescription can cause personal pain and suffering.

Too often, we compare ourselves to others. If there is any comparison in our lives, it should be to those who are less fortunate. It should involve reflecting on how we can alleviate their suffering through our gifts. Or your comparison should be to recognize that another person has found the way to be more compassionate, more loving, more patient, more tolerant, more humble, or more forgiving than you are.

We rarely see the world through these perspectives. But this sort of outlook can free us from greed and frustration. Too often, we assess character based on title, power, and possessions. None of these issues speak to character. Character is based on free will and choice. To understand someone's character, you must understand that person's value system. Our values define our character and guide our words and actions.

Contentment also protects us from unethical behavior. We lose the tendency to make decisions based on greed. We no longer pursue unethical courses to achieve excessive materialistic goals. Happiness can never result from greed, jealousy, or dishonesty. With contentment, we can pursue an altruistic path. The happiness and peace that comes from contentment allows us to smile, laugh, and dance in the world.

Personally, I needed to acquire more gratitude for the blessings and gifts that God had given me. I had to stop comparing myself to others who had more. I now appreciate the fact that I enjoy much more opportunity than millions of other people. Keeping this in mind ignites in me a sense of gratitude and perspective. I have also realized that by following Mother Teresa's prescription, I will acquire what God desired me to have—no less and no more.

Mother Teresa lived by this attitude toward divine providence. I have visited many homes of the Missionaries of Charity throughout the world. The sisters live in simple surroundings. They own a pair of sandals, two saris, and rosary beads. These are their sole possessions. They do not own property or equipment. They have no desire to gain more. Nor do they compare themselves and what they have to others. If they do, such comparisons heighten their compassion and love for those who are less fortunate and in need of service.

Contentment is a quality tied to the moment. To feel it, one must give up worry about the future and the circumstances we cannot control. "Take whatever God gives and surrender whatever he takes with a big smile," Mother Teresa said. She was content with the consequences of her actions, knowing that she was doing God's work. This did not mean that she did not desire more. It is important to differentiate between the concept of contentment and the concept of desire. Mother Teresa always wanted more—more men and women in the order, more homes for the poor throughout the world.

For the two years before she died in 1997, she had the sisters constantly pray for her intentions in China. She was always motivated to achieve more, but the more was not for herself but for God and humanity. She knew her purpose. She thought about life and reacted with her beautiful prescription. It addresses external situations and circumstances and accepts the consequences with peace. Mother Teresa was content, knowing the results were in God's hands.

SOMETHING TO CONSIDER . . .

1. What are your material goals, the things you want, the lifestyle you hope to have? How much time do you spend thinking about or working to achieve these goals? Is it too much time?
2. What things would you give up to fully incorporate contentment and gratitude into your life?

CHAPTER 16 Faith

Contentment and knowing that the consequences of our actions are in God's hands leads us to the element of faith.

Many times I tried to ask Mother Teresa how she was feeling physically. She would always dismiss my question by saying, "There's not enough time to talk about it. There is too much work." If I persisted, she would respond, "I am fine. Yesterday is gone, tomorrow has not yet come. We have only today to love and serve; let us begin." She was absolutely convinced that God has a plan, and that our responsibility is to love, serve, and leave the consequences to God. This is the essence of faith.

In Mother Teresa, I saw a beautiful happiness, peace, and serenity. I have not seen this in anyone else in my life. It was a peace and serenity that stemmed from her realization that she was serving God and doing God's work. She had a knowledge that freed her from worry about the consequences of her decisions. She also knew that if she made a mistake, asking for forgiveness would bring forgiveness from God. What a wonderful way to free yourself from a mountain of misery, fear, guilt, and regret.

Because Mother Teresa lived by divine providence, she recognized that God does not go bankrupt. Nor does he make mistakes. God either allowed things to happen or wanted them to happen, even though we are not capable of understanding all of his reasons. She did not worry about tomorrow. To her, the future was in God's hands, and she surrendered herself to his will. Indeed, she did not even worry about the future of her order. She believed that if her missionaries kept doing God's work and if God wished them to continue that work, the order would thrive.

Her only concern was doing God's work. That meant serving the poorest of the poor, alleviating their hunger, loneliness, and nakedness in all its forms. Others' reactions to her work did not worry her either. She oversaw a religious order serving hundreds of thousands of poor people in more than 120 countries. She herself, however, had no financial reserves. She trusted solely in God's will and had faith that he would supply her with the support and materials she needed. If God did not wish it, she believed, he would not sustain her mission. "If God wants the work, God will provide the resources. He will not go bankrupt."

When we are contemplating a problem, we tend to base our decisions on what we think will be the best personal result. Mother Teresa did not use this method. Instead, her motto was, "All for Jesus." She would say, "If it's not for Jesus, it's not worth doing." Another time, she summed it up this way: "We are not called to be successful; we are called to be faithful."

She maintained this intense faith even though she personally saw more human suffering—the results of hatred, anger, and greed—than perhaps any person who has ever lived. If I saw such human tragedies on such a constant basis, I think it would weaken my faith. God has given me so much—so much opportunity, so much potential—and my personal sacrifices for humanity have been nothing compared to hers. When I experience personal loss, for example, I ask God why he let this happen to me. I have questioned God's love for me. This happened when I wanted progress on programs for the poor and underserved and my prayers consistently went unanswered. I asked myself: Is this not God's work? Now, with the help of Mother's prescription, I have learned to ask, meditate, or pray not for the success of a program or project, but for the strength to accept the consequences and God's will for my efforts. Faith allows us to accept what otherwise would be emotionally impossible.

Mother Teresa endured tests of faith just as we all do. How could she maintain such a faith with all this human destruction around her and with her requests for help often delayed or denied? I might say, "I've given everything for you, God. Why do you make this so difficult?" To me, periodic spiritual weakness would simply be human, regardless of how holy, faithful, or saintly a person would be. Consequently, I was not surprised to learn that she had periods of "inner darkness." The Roman Catholic Church acknowledged this inner darkness as a saintly characteristic. Pope John Paul II made note of it in his homily for Mother Teresa's beatification.

"Mother Teresa shared in the passion of the crucifixion of Christ in a special way during her years of 'inner darkness,'" he said. "For her that was a test, at times an agonizing one, which she accepted as a rare 'gift.' In the darkest hours, she clung even more tenaciously to prayer before the Blessed Sacrament. The harsh spiritual trial led her to identify herself more and more closely with those she served each day, feeling their pain, and at times, even their rejection. She was fond of repeating that the greatest poverty is to be unwanted, to have no one to take care of you. How often, like a psalmist, Mother Teresa called to her Lord in times of inner desolation: 'In you I hope, my God.'" For Mother Teresa, these tests only strengthened her faith.

I once asked Mother Teresa what someone with no faith or weak faith should do to stay on the path of service, compassion, and love. I can sum up her answer by quoting from what she called her "business card." It was the little piece of paper she handed out by the dozens to the people she met. I keep the one she gave me as my road map of faith. It states: "The fruit of silence is prayer; the fruit of prayer is faith; the fruit of faith is love; the fruit of love is service; the fruit of service is peace."

SOMETHING TO CONSIDER . . .

1. When in your life has your faith weakened? What were the circumstances? Where did you turn to restore your faith? Were you successful?
2. How would your life change if you were to put yourself and the consequences of your actions in God's hands?

CHAPTER 17 Humility

Mother Teresa's humility was profound. She did not enjoy giving interviews. Nor did she desire the Nobel Peace Prize, but she accepted it "in the name of all those who feel unwanted, unloved, rejected by society, or who are a burden to society or are excluded." She accepted awards to bring a new understanding between the rich and poor and an awareness of the poor throughout the world.

My bishop once asked me what Mother Teresa was like as a person. Some of her critics have characterized her as remote and unapproachable. I replied that she required community to nurture her, but that she did not keep herself isolated. In public, she walked freely, smiled at everyone, blessed everyone, and talked to everyone she could. And when she spoke to someone, she had the gift of making that person feel that he or she was the only one she was concerned about. Someone's title or wealth was of no importance to Mother Teresa. In chapel, for example, she would never sit next to the most important person in the room. It did not matter to her who knelt beside her or who shared her prayer book.

Mother Teresa had none of that excessive preoccupation with position and power that destroys self-contentment. She believed that titles or positions of leadership should be used to support and serve others. They should not be ends in themselves to bolster one's pride and ego.

Many years ago when I was a resident, an older psychiatrist, whom I will call "Charles," would occasionally see me in the cafeteria and sit with me over a cup of coffee. Many younger doctors considered Charles to be out of touch with current medical trends. He spent a great deal of time in talk therapy with his patients at a time when drug therapy was growing in popularity. I was one of those colleagues who would not make up an excuse to leave when he entered the cafeteria or doctors lounge.

One day, he invited me to his house, and I reluctantly agreed to go. He lived alone, and the first thing I noticed in his house were the many squares on the wallpaper where frames had once hung. I asked Charles where the pictures had gone and he took me to his basement door. He had removed all his degrees, honorary degrees, and award certificates from their frames, folded them into paper airplanes, and flew them down the basement stairs, one by one. He tried to fling each one farther than the last. It had become a game for him.

Why had Charles done this? Charles told me that all those symbols of his power and prestige came to mean nothing to him. His drive to obtain them had caused him much personal loss. His focus on work and materialistic advantages, titles, and prestige had cost him his wife and children many years earlier. In the end, he also lost his professional prestige and relationships that had kept him in good standing in the medical community. His younger colleagues saw him as irrelevant, and no one was interested in publishing his papers or hearing his thoughts at conferences. He had realized his mistakes too late. All he could do now was turn his meaningless honors into paper airplanes.

At the time I went to Charles's home, I was a young resident. I did not understand the message Charles had for me. I presumed that he was merely an eccentric physician who was bitter about the losses in both his personal and professional life. As for me, I was part of the cardiology department. It was rapidly becoming the most important and lucrative department at our hospital. That gave doctors like me power and influence within our community and the promise of wealth and prestige in the future.

Later, I met Mother Teresa and witnessed her enormous humility. This was a woman who wielded great world influence. When I reflected on my experience with Charles, I saw what he had been trying to tell me. Be careful, control your ego and your desire for power, recognition, and authority. If you don't, it will control and destroy the things that matter in your life and will ultimately destroy you.

Charles was an example of how ego and desire for personal power can create devastating losses. Controlling those desires can help guide you toward achieving inner peace and happiness. If you have personal or professional desires, you do not have to abandon them. Plan to improve your life within reason. Discipline your mind to accept whatever is given and whatever is taken away. The knowledge that God loves you and guides your life will free you from worry, stress, and anxiety.

I must communicate daily with my employees, partners, patients, insurance company representatives, and hospital administrators. Frequently, their focus and ultimate decisions on an issue may not be the same as mine. I ask myself if I have been fair with that individual. I remind myself that while not everyone will agree with me, my responsibility is to be compassionate to another's concerns, frustrations, and sufferings. I must present myself with humility, without aggression or anger, and be willing to forgive any results that seem contrary to my purpose. Achieving these goals allows me to maintain my dignity and sense that I am following Mother's prescription.

When someone does come to you for advice, see it as an opportunity to develop empathy. Thus, if you do experience the pain of unjust criticism or condemnation, you know you did the best you could do. As Mother Teresa would say, "If you are humble, nothing will touch you."

Have humility, so that whatever criticism does come your way, it will not destroy your inner peace and happiness. If your humility is powerful enough, any criticism will not affect you. Make sure that your focus is one of compassion and service. Accept criticism and its consequences with peace, knowing that the ultimate consequences are not in your hands and that your actions came from a sincere desire to help another. You will protect yourself from the sting of unjust criticism if your intentions are consistent with the prescription. You will know that you acted with the goal of alleviating suffering. If your focus in mind, word, and action are incompatible with the prescription, it will be difficult to justify your actions. In this case, any pain or suffering you experience is self-inflicted and might even be expected.

Mother Teresa had an intense sense of self-confidence and certainty that she was doing God's work because she had such certainty about the purpose of life. On one of my visits with her, I asked her about this. I still have her answer written down on a tablet. It is all about humility. She said, "We have been sent to serve and not to be served. We must serve with a humble heart. We must share what we have with a humble heart. Dedicate yourself without reservation; give of yourself generously and unconditionally."

SOMETHING TO CONSIDER . . .

1. How do you react when others disagree with your ideas or suggestions?
2. Do you expect others around you to adapt to your needs and desires?
3. Are there times in your life when you have played the role of a servant, "the least of these"?

CHAPTER 18 Tolerance

Mother Teresa did not judge others. Everyone who desired to help was welcome in her houses, even if that person's reputation was questionable. She welcomed all because by doing so she brought people closer to God and helped them to fulfill God's call to serve. By showing them how to serve and grow in love and compassion, she was doing God's work and increasing awareness of the need to serve the poorest of the poor. At the same time, her tolerance meant she did not have to waste time and energy on judging whether she should accept someone's offer to help.

Instead, Mother Teresa looked to God for guidance. She told me, "God works in his own way in the heart of each person. We can never know how close another human being is to God; therefore, we must not judge or condemn that person. The only thing that really counts is that we love."

In the 1990s, Mother decided to open a home for AIDS patients in New York City. The role that homosexual activity plays in the transmission of AIDS and the fact that the Catholic church condemns homosexual activity was of no concern to her. "We are not here to sit in judgment of these people, or to decide blame or guilt or sin," she said. "Our mission is to help them, and to make their dying days more tolerable." Her sole focus was on alleviating suffering. That was the purpose of her life. She saw a need and filled it.

Mother Teresa also went outside her community to teach the purpose of life. She did not choose a cloistered life, but one that consistently brought her into contact with the outside world and its diverse people. Many of these people opposed her values, thoughts, and attitudes. She had patience and tolerance for all of these people because of her calling to share her wisdom and her message of compassion and love. When people came to her for advice, she did not think about their skin color, religious beliefs, or political views. Instead, she saw humanity and God within that humanity. She remembered her call to relieve suffering. There were people like me who did not need food, drink, or clothing. We needed wisdom. She freely gave that wisdom to all.

Tolerance seemed to come easily to Mother Teresa. For most of us, however, it is a complex issue. Obviously, we must respect every life, regardless of nationality, creed, origin, or any of the other qualities that make each of us unique. Often that tolerance is difficult, but it helps to remember that Christ is in each of us, as Mother Teresa said.

An attitude of tolerance becomes more challenging when someone else's values, lifestyle, or attitudes thwart our pursuit of life's purpose. How much tolerance should you show that person? If you are involved with people, activities, or environments that are not helping you to live out your calling, you cannot continue in that way. You must break free of whoever and whatever keeps you from your purpose of life. You are not condemning or judging that person. You are rejecting that person's attempt to achieve peace or happiness through dysfunctional means, such as the pursuit of power or excessive material wealth. Or, you are turning away from their efforts to keep you from pursuing your purpose in life. One example of this might be an abusive spouse who controls the other spouse's life through fear or violence. Another might be the recovering substance abuser who finds himself or herself tempted by friendships with other addicts.

Instead, you should find strength among those who support your pursuit of Mother Teresa's prescription. Remember that commitment to community. Find others who will support and nurture you, within your church, volunteer group, or family.

If Mother Teresa showed any intolerance, it was toward those who committed injustices against the poor. I saw this firsthand when the U.S. Air Force failed to deliver the entire shipment of clothing to Mother Teresa's Calcutta missions. (This was described in an earlier chapter.) Mother Teresa was vocal about her displeasure that some of the boxes on the manifest did not arrive. She talked of a government investigation to discover who might have taken what she considered "gifts for Jesus." Mother Teresa could not tolerate the idea that someone would steal from the poor.

We must ask ourselves how often we steal from the poor. Do we deny them proper health care because of their inability to pay? Do we fail to provide clothing, housing, and social support? Our capabilities and knowledge are gifts from God. Do we have a right to force payment from those who cannot pay? Can we justify letting our brothers and sisters suffer simply because they do not have the required money? Do we have a right to send people into bankruptcy, to deny them legal aid, to refuse medication or treatment, or to cut off telephone, gas, or electric services? These actions may not constitute stealing directly, but delayed services become services denied. Isn't that just another, intolerable way of stealing from the poor?

Mother Teresa believed that when the poor die of thirst, hunger, or lack of appropriate health care, it is not because God failed to care for them. It is because other people chose not to be the instruments of God's love and compassion. We do not care enough to distribute these resources appropriately to alleviate the suffering of others. Our lack of compassion causes these social injustices that Mother Teresa found so intolerable.

SOMETHING TO CONSIDER . . .

1. Have you judged someone today? What was the issue or issues? How could you have adapted an attitude of tolerance to make the situation better?
2. Are there situations in your life or community where the poor are being denied services? What could you do to help?

CHAPTER 19 Patience

Mother Teresa was always patient with those who desired knowledge from her. She knew that people are not only hungry for food but also for wisdom. She realized that many people, like me, sought her out for knowledge and illumination. Her duty and desire was to feed them, even though they were often wealthy in material goods.

Mother Teresa is best known for her service to those suffering from physical poverty. However, she was not always successful in opening homes for the poor in every country or location she desired. There were times when she wanted to open leprosy homes, but the communities where they were to be located rejected the plan. For most of us, such rejection would be difficult to take. Mother Teresa accepted such setbacks with patience. Her belief was that if God wanted the work, God would provide the resources. That thought always sustained her. If he did not provide the resources, he did not want the work to develop at that time.

Remember this when attempting to acquire the patience to survive disappointments. There are people, institutions, and organizations that may not desire to support such programs. If the resources cannot be obtained through these sources, then God does not desire the work at this time. We must accept his will and move forward, filled with peace.

For me, this has been a difficult concept to accept. Many times, I have spent time and effort attempting to convince decisionmakers that a particular program or action would benefit the poor, only to be rejected for financial or political reasons. Or, the "no" may have come simply because these people were not interested.

Mother Teresa was impatient with people who wasted time or resources. On one occasion, Mother Teresa found out that a woman in Calcutta suffering from leprosy was not taking her medications consistently. Leprosy is a contagious disease but the contagious phase can be suppressed and even cured with appropriate therapy. The medications, however, are quite expensive. Mother Teresa confronted the woman. This was the only time I ever saw Mother scold another person. She approached the woman, pursed her lips together, and explained that the medications were a rare commodity. She told the woman that if she did not truly desire proper therapy, then she should respect others who would use the medications correctly. Mother Teresa did not yell or denigrate the woman, but she spoke seriously, disciplining her as a mother would her child.

We may also grow impatient to accomplish too much, too fast. I recall one occasion when I told Mother Teresa about my efforts and intentions. I asked her if I was truly doing enough in God's eyes. Was I serving enough? Was I sacrificing enough?

Mother Teresa felt a certain sense of disappointment that the work she was doing was only a "drop in the ocean." You may feel that way about your efforts to alleviate the suffering of others. Like her, you should receive satisfaction knowing that you are doing God's work and that the ocean benefits from every drop you—and others like you—add to it.

Mother Teresa also realized that time was very valuable and she sometimes reminded those around her, "Too much talk; we must start to work." She was not one to spend a great deal of time in committee meetings or organizational meetings. In that setting neither she nor her sisters were closely involved in one-on-one relationships with the poor.

Mother Teresa realized that time was very valuable, but she was invariably patient with people. Here, she greets and makes time to talk and joke with Maria Alana Wright, then fourteen years old. Patience is one of the ten attitudes of spirit prescribed by Mother Teresa.

I can allow the pressures and the stress to become overwhelming when I arrive at work each morning and look over my patient list. Then, I realize that I have been doing this for more than twenty years. My patient management is good. I have enough faith in my knowledge and capabilities to know that I can alleviate suffering and yet be patient enough to take one case at a time.

The same is true in your life. Do not be impatient to accomplish everything at once. Mother Teresa based her life on doing small things with great love—every day. When you concentrate on doing the same, think of how your acts of compassion and love will add up over the days, weeks, months, and years. As Mother Teresa said, "We can feed only one patient at a time. We can treat only one patient at a time. We can resolve issues only one at a time." Having the patience to follow her wisdom is the difficult part.

SOMETHING TO CONSIDER . . .

1. How would you rate your ability to be patient in difficult circumstances? Very patient? Somewhat patient? Not patient at all?
2. How do you show your impatience? Are you impatient with others, yourself, with both?
3. Are you ready or willing to patiently adapt Mother Teresa's prescription for happiness and peace? Which of the spiritual attitudes recommended by Mother Teresa is the best starting point for you?

CHAPTER 20 Forgiveness

Mother Teresa nurtured the value of forgiveness, both in herself and in her Missionaries of Charity. Her coworkers also had the opportunity to experience her loving forgiveness. By the time I met Mother Teresa, she had received the Nobel Peace Prize and major awards from governments around the world. Millions—not just Christians but also Muslims, Jews, Buddhists, and Hindus—recognized her as a powerful spiritual force.

One would think that this type of international recognition would give Mother Teresa the right to be angry or unforgiving toward world leaders who could do so much to alleviate suffering in their countries. The contrary was true. She believed that any contact she had with these leaders helped to make them and the world more aware of the need to serve the poor and to teach the purpose of life.

Mother Teresa could also be forgiving in the face of the harshest attacks on her character. I recall one time in 1994 in Calcutta when British television aired a program that aggressively criticized Mother Teresa's methods and activities. I saw the transcript of this program that someone had sent to the motherhouse. Reading it, I felt a sense of outrage that I had rarely experienced before. Mother Teresa emerged from a private meeting about the program, and we all waited to hear her reaction and her plan to respond publicly.

What she had to say was full of forgiveness: "Our work is God's work. If God wishes the work, he shall provide the resources. If he does not, then he does not desire the work. All is forgiven. Yesterday is gone, tomorrow has not yet come, we have only today to love and serve. Let us begin."

Her response did not heal my anger or sense of injustice, and I told her this. She looked at me—not with the customary kind smile, but with the pursed lips that showed she was concentrating on a difficult issue. She said, "Dr. Paul, you must rid yourself of this anger. You need to pray more—there is much work to be done." Then she walked away to do just that.

I stopped to think how I would have reacted without her advice. If an enemy had aimed such attacks at me, I would have summoned my lawyers, filed a lawsuit, and been consumed for months, or even years, with revenge. In the process, I would have lost sight of my true purpose of life, distracted by my need for revenge and vindication. Mother Teresa, on the other hand, never lost focus on her purpose to serve the poorest of the poor. She was never concerned with how others perceived her and what they said about her, lies or not. This attitude set her free to do God's work without interruption.

"You can be happy and at peace in this world, but you must love as he loved. You must think as he thought, you must act as he acted, you must forgive as he forgave," she said.

You may have someone in your life toward whom you feel resentment or anger. It may be a relative or a friend from whom you are estranged because of a misunderstanding. It could be a former business associate who may have cheated you out of money, an ex-spouse who walked out on your marriage. Your inability to forgive that person is consuming your spiritual energy and preventing you from realizing fully your purpose of life. Apply what Mother Teresa said, and think of how Christ would have forgiven that person. Reach out and say—either directly to the person or in your own heart—"I forgive you." In this way, you free yourself to achieve your purpose in life.

Mother Teresa tried to follow Jesus every day. The words and forgiving example of Jesus will set you free. It requires great humility to forgive easily. Mother Teresa believed and lived out the idea that if you are humble enough, no praise or criticism will affect you. Let nothing draw your attention from the work of serving others. "All is forgiven."

SOMETHING TO CONSIDER . . .

1. Whom do you need to forgive in your life? How could you go about doing it? What first steps would you take in approaching the person you want to forgive?
2. Are there people in your life from whom you could seek forgiveness? Why? How would you approach those people?

CHAPTER 21 Honesty

Mother Teresa had to make the final decision on issues involving a religious order serving in more than 120 countries. Some of these countries had up to twenty houses each. These decisions had to be made even though languages, customs, and laws were extremely varied. Some countries were officially atheistic, while others were predominantly Jewish, Christian, Muslim, or Hindu. Still, Mother Teresa was capable of making the right decision, maintaining respect for all faiths, and transcending religious and political boundaries.

The reason is part of the prescription. She was honest. She was not caught up in the pressure to be "politically correct" or to say what others wanted to hear so that they would think well of her. She never worried about the consequences of any of her decisions.

Once, meeting with her in New York, I asked her what she based her decisions on. Her response was, "All for Jesus."

Mother Teresa was called to leadership, but she adopted a simplicity of focus that some criticized as not socially active enough. She was a Roman Catholic nun called to leave the comforts of the private academy in which she was teaching. She traveled to the slums of Calcutta to serve the poorest of the poor, and she presented herself honestly and simply through that calling.

The best example I can give of her honesty occurred at the National Prayer Breakfast in Washington, D.C., on February 3, 1994. President Clinton had asked Mother Teresa to speak. The audience was full of politicians and pro-abortion VIPs, including the president, vice president, and their wives. Mother Teresa was not intimidated. In her speech, she spoke honestly about her respect for all human life and the need to protect and preserve that life. She told these leaders that the "unborn child had been carved in the hand of God from conception." She called on them to make America "a sign of peace for the world" by caring for the "weakest of the weak—the unborn child."

Mother Teresa did not mean to insult or demean anyone with her speech. Her intent was not to burn bridges with American leaders. (In fact, she did not. Hillary and Chelsea Clinton visited one of Mother's homes in Calcutta a year after the prayer breakfast, and Mrs. Clinton helped Mother open an orphanage in Washington in 1995. In 1997 Mrs. Clinton attended Mother's funeral.) Mother's intent was to teach and remind us all of our responsibilities to respect human life. She was confident that people would be open to hearing her message, and that some, if not all, might learn from it.

I sat down to talk with Mother Teresa a couple of days later in Washington. She asked me what I thought of the speech. "Mother, it certainly was not a politically correct speech, but it was very beautiful," I told her. She smiled and said, "I did not come to Washington to be politically correct, but to teach and speak the truth."

Shortly after her speech in Washington, her sisters were concerned about Mother's health and asked me to check her blood pressure. I asked her how she was feeling, and as usual, she would not give a direct response. She merely smiled and said, "Too much work to think about it." She raised the sleeve of her sari on her right arm. Just as I was about to inflate the blood pressure cuff, she said, "Please do not worry my children. If my blood pressure is a little high, please let us keep this between Jesus, you, and me."

Thank God her blood pressure that day was normal. Sister after sister approached me to ask what the reading had shown. It would not have been easy for me to be evasive with such loving individuals so concerned about their Mother.

The sisters were motivated by compassion and love. More often, however, we face demands from people who seek only profit and are untouched by compassion. I find it better to avoid these folks. This may be a sign of weakness on my part, but in most instances, they are unhappy and focused on using others for their own advancement.

Occasionally, I must deal with these people. This is where honesty becomes important. Sometimes I must attend a meeting with people whose direction and perspective are very different from mine. The atmosphere may be one of anger or greed, as the different parties vie to gain position. I am always concerned that I may become angry as well or that I might insult someone by speaking my mind. Then I realize my responsibility is one of honesty, conveyed with compassion and humility. If I express my beliefs with hostility or aggression, the same attitude will be directed at me. On the other hand, if I am afraid to speak honestly, then I cannot expect others to deal honestly with me.

Honesty, like the other elements of the prescription, has its consequences. If my colleagues do not wish to call me back to future meetings, that is fine. If they wish to respect my opinion and perhaps alter their own direction, that, to me, is a good result. If they wish to disregard my focus, I know that my intention was not to offend anyone. I have attempted to resolve the conflict in an honest, compassionate, tolerant, and forgiving manner. I can leave the meeting and its issues behind me, while the others continue to argue, mistrust, and manipulate one another.

People will often come to you with ideas or proposals that you consider contrary to your purpose in life. It is not your responsibility to convince them to agree with you. People will do what they want regardless of your opinion or advice. The comfort comes in addressing them honestly and with humility. You are obligated to share your wisdom; your conscience cannot be imprisoned. This allows you to maintain inner peace and happiness. Yes, their suffering might be alleviated if they accept your advice. But chances are they will not. Recognize that they are confused and lost, and are hungry for your wisdom. Like you, they are struggling to find peace and happiness, but they may be attempting to reach those goals in nonfunctional ways.

Often, our self-interest—the fear of losing power, a friend, or a business advantage—prevents us from recognizing and acting on the truth. Or, we speak the truth only when it advances our self-interest. This happens often in the area of human rights. In our country's history, many Americans tolerated slavery because it gave the South an economic advantage. It was easier for people in the North to call for the end of slavery because they were not benefiting as directly from such an immoral system. Unfortunately for our nation, it took the Civil War to end slavery. Had more people given up their self-interest, admitted the truth, and then acted to make things right, much bloodshed might have been avoided. When you want nothing for yourself, you are no longer blind to "invisible" injustices and can start to see ways to right them.

There have been times in my life when I have been blind to injustice and failed to speak the truth. In the town where I grew up, Steubenville, Ohio, we had several public swimming pools. We called one of them the "Ink Well," a small, run-down, dirty pool where the town's blacks were expected to swim. I was a lifeguard at one of the better pools in a white neighborhood. In the summer, my friends and I enjoyed swimming. My black friends always went to the Ink Well and we went to "our" pool. I accepted this arrangement without a thought. Now, I realize that I allowed myself to be blind to the inferior treatment my friends and other blacks received. I did not speak out because, perhaps unconsciously, I knew it would have cost me my valuable summer income.

In my professional world today, I see injustice in the inadequate health care available to underinsured or uninsured Americans. This injustice exists because those in power refuse to stand up and become advocates for those who cannot change the system. Many involved in the health care profession do not speak the truth because it is in their self-interest to maintain the status quo in the form of profits. Changes will not occur unless they act to make medical care accessible to all, regardless of the person's ability to pay. Perhaps someday we will have an honest debate, unsullied by political and corporate doublespeak, on this important ethical and moral issue.

SOMETHING TO CONSIDER . . .

1. Think of an incident in which you did not express your true feelings but wanted to. Were you trying to be "politically correct"? What would have happened had you been honest? Could you have accepted the consequences?

CHAPTER 22 A Life of Service

A few years ago, my family and I took a vacation to Alaska, and one of the highlights I enjoyed was the chance to drive a dogsled. There were ten dogs on my sled, including the lead dog, "Blondie." This dog had been part of a team that had won the famous Iditarod race.

As the dogs jumped and pranced at their leads, anxious to run, I nervously listened to the handlers explain what I should do. They warned me, "These dogs can take you over a rock-strewn glacier or through a ravine. They can also take you on the smoothest ride of a lifetime." The key, they said, was to choose the proper dogs, position them properly, and discipline yourself and your team to focus on reaching your destination. They advised me to concentrate on the lead dog and never lose sight of her. Take your eye off Blondie, the guides said, and you risk crashing.

Looking back on that adventure, I see it as a metaphor for Mother Teresa's message and prescription. The lead dog is like the purpose of life. The other dogs are the components of my prescription. I ask myself, "What is my lead dog? What is my purpose in life?" Mother Teresa had given me the answer for my sled ride through life the first time I met her. She told me to dedicate my life to serving others. The ten spiritual attitudes that complete the prescription followed along as I kept my eye on that purpose.

When I touch a human being who is poor, naked, sick, homeless, or thirsty, I am touching Christ in the distressing disguise of the poor. In my practice, I never deny people an appointment based on their finances. The only criteria are urgency and need of care. To me, this confirms my true purpose of life and my responsibility to humanity, especially the poor. It cements Mother Teresa's influence on me as I try to live according to her prescription.

The biggest change in my life is the one that occurred within me, not the outside changes that others might see. Mother Teresa's wisdom and example transformed me. Medical advances allow physicians like me to help the blind see and the lame walk. But we have not found a way to alter someone's purpose in life to one of service. To me that is the most difficult miracle of all to perform. Mother Teresa has fostered this miracle in countless people throughout the world. She continues to do so after her death. To me, this is what makes her a saint. This is a true miracle.

I continue to practice cardiology in Youngstown and Warren, Ohio, but my focus now is on alleviating the suffering of my patients. I am called simply to do that. I still work twelve- to fourteen-hour days. I am on call every third night and every other weekend. These are demanding hours, but now that I am older, I find great satisfaction in dedicating myself to my patients rather than to professional or material rewards. I see fewer patients because fulfilling elements of the prescription, such as compassion, patience, and tolerance, requires me to reject the model of the hurried, impersonal office "exam." The poor are treated without charge, and the underinsured pay what they can afford. I enjoy being a doctor now more than I ever have because I serve for *someone* rather than for *something*. Medicine is no longer just a business for me.

I have also discovered that I require fewer things to make me happy. The dream house I planned on building years ago is forgotten. My wife and I have no need for a bigger home. We still live in the ranch home my parents bought more than thirty-five years ago. My daughter is now a preschool teacher. My detachment from material things allows me to focus on and enjoy my work.

I allow myself time for other activities that serve my purpose of life. The clothing mission continues every month, and the medication programs in Trumbull and Mahoning counties are continuing to grow. I am working with Notre Dame alumni on forming similar medication programs in their communities. My leadership activities are limited as well. I recognized long ago that I am not wired to be an administrator or a hospital department chair. However, I am a member of the Catholic Diocese of Youngstown board of trustees, which focuses on the poor and underserved, and am on the St. Joseph Hospital Foundation board, which concentrates on community health care needs.

In 2004 I developed a medical ethics program that will be held every semester for one weekend for Notre Dame students who are interested in health careers. We speak about issues such as the purpose of the profession, compassion, and how to maintain a sense of inner peace. This is a way to serve my profession and help future physicians and others in the medical arts learn about Mother Teresa's message and prescription for peace and happiness.

I do not see myself ever stopping these activities. They are intimately tied to my purpose of life and my spiritual happiness and peace. Retirement in the traditional sense is not an option. Can we ever retire from giving ourselves to others? So often as soon as we can afford to retire, we do so and take all our knowledge and experience with us. Are we not obligated instead to continue to serve as long as we are physically and mentally capable of doing so?

We may think this is a difficult path, but consider the example of the late Pope John Paul II. I was in Rome for the pontiff's twenty-fifth anniversary celebration. During the Mass in St. Peter's Square, he said that all of us must serve humanity. He said that God had chosen him to lead the church and that he would continue as long as God wanted him to do so. I was impressed that even with all his obvious physical discomforts, he maintained his demanding schedule, constantly giving of himself until his death in April 2005.

Mother Teresa also understood that self-sacrifice is constant. Her responsibilities in later years became greater. At the same time, her physical strength began to falter. She suffered from several chronic illnesses: heart problems, arthritis, vision problems, and bouts of malaria. Yet she maintained a daily schedule that would have exhausted someone much younger. She seemed to run on prayer. She would retire to her chapel and emerge revitalized, sustained by the belief that she was accomplishing God's work.

Mother Teresa voluntarily surrendered her personal life completely to the service of humanity. She not only made herself poor but also a servant to the poor. As she often said, "The mantle that hides a life of self-sacrifice is a life of joy and happiness." If we hesitate to embrace a life of self-sacrifice and lose our faith that God will take care of us, then we deny ourselves the opportunities for peace and happiness that God desires for us.

SOMETHING TO CONSIDER . . .

1. How do you see yourself living out the prescription one year, five years, ten years from now? How will your life be different?

EPILOGUE

Mother Teresa's Final Advice

I once asked Mother Teresa what advice she would give to her Missionaries of Charity when they felt discouraged.

Mother said, "When one feels empty, lonely, weak, then that's the time one must go on one's knees."

When I feel overloaded by personal or professional demands, when I feel extreme limitation of time, when more emergencies come to the hospital than expected, when I am pulled between requests from insurance companies, attorneys, hospital administrators, colleagues, patients, and family members, I do not literally go to my knees. But I do allow my mind to take me back to a small, hot, humid room in a nondescript building outside Tijuana, Mexico. I close my eyes and once again listen to Mother's message about the purpose of life.

I feel happiest when I have disciplined myself to become unselfish, focusing only on the welfare of others and alleviating suffering with no consideration for my own gain. This is when I am truly fulfilling my purpose in life. When I do not do this, I am susceptible to the negative forces of greed, anger, jealousy, materialism, and others that breed unhappiness. When I suppress these negative forces, I can grow in compassion, contentment, humility, tolerance, and all the other elements of Mother's prescription. I find myself happy and spiritually at peace.

Our challenge is to grow closer to God by doing works of compassion and love that alleviate others' suffering. No matter what your faith, the foundation of the prescription must be love and compassion. Once we recognize this, we can achieve peace and happiness by doing God's work. Accepting Mother

Teresa's message and applying her prescription to your life is not a simple matter. It requires an intense passion for personal transformation, a fundamental change in the way you view the world and your place in it.

When Mother Teresa gave me her message so many years ago, it was only an abstract idea. For me, the beauty has been taking that concept and turning it into a way of living that worked for me. It is one that can be taken anywhere, used by anyone, whatever the circumstances may be.

Jesus said, "Peace be with you, my peace I give to you." Mother Teresa took those words and showed me how to bring peace into my life. She did it by showing me the purpose of life and how to carry it out. Mother did not begin a revolution of love and compassion; Jesus did that. Mother's miracle is that she lived a life of love and compassion and, through it, gave the world a message and a prescription for sustained peace and happiness, if only we would observe her and follow her examples. Her revolution was to increase the world's awareness of the poor and suffering. Her message and prescription can heal us. If you face every day with her prescription, you will heal wounds and injuries from the past and prevent an enormous amount of future injuries, suffering, and pain.

Your future peace of mind, happiness, and closeness to God depend upon you and your reaction to the outside world. Mother's prescription gives you the power to set aside the hurt of others' criticism and give up the fear of loss of power, title, or prestige, or the need to keep up with others' expectations. The choice is yours.

The last question I ever asked Mother was how I could become a better physician. She answered, "Don't ever forget whom you are touching." That person is Christ, your brother or sister in the distressing disguise of the poor. Serve that person with compassion. This is your purpose in life, your obligation. This is how you will be judged.

APPENDIX 1 Houses of the Missionaries of Charity in North America

United States

Arkansas
LITTLE ROCK
1014 S. Oak St.
Little Rock, AR 72204
1-501-633-3596

Arizona
PHOENIX
1414 S. 17th Ave.
Phoenix, AZ 85007
1-602-258-5504

California
LOS ANGELES
10950 California Ave.
Lynwood, CA 90262
1-310-635-3264

PACIFICA
Gift of Love
164 Milagra Dr.
Pacifica, CA 94044
1-650-355-3091

SAN FRANCISCO
Queen of Peace
55 Sadowa St.
San Francisco, CA 94112
415-586-3449

SAN FRANCISCO
Novitiate
312 29th St.
San Francisco, CA 94131
1-415-647-1889

Colorado
DENVER
1340 Grant St.
Denver, CO 80203
1-303-860-8040

Connecticut
BRIDGEPORT
599 Beechwood Ave.
Bridgeport, CT 06604
1-203-336-5626

Georgia
ATLANTA
995 St. Charles Ave.
Atlanta, GA 30306
1-404-892-5111

Illinois
CHICAGO
2234 West Washington Blvd.
Chicago, IL 60612
1-312-421-0038

PEORIA
506 Hancock St.
Peoria, IL 61603
1-309-674-7160

Indiana
GARY
509 W. Ridge Rd.
Gary, IN 46408
1-219-884-2140

INDIANAPOLIS
2424 E. 10th St.
Indianapolis, IN 46201
1-317-916-6753

Kentucky
JENKINS
44 Cove Rd.
P.O, Box 883
Jenkins, KT 41557
1-606-832-4824

Louisiana
BATON ROUGE
737 East Blvd.
Baton Rouge, LA 70802
1-225-383-8367

LAFAYETTE
911 St. John's St.
Lafayette, LA 70501
1-318-233-3929

Maryland
BALTIMORE
Gift of Hope
818 Collington Ave.
Baltimore, MD 21205
1-410-732-6056

Massachusetts
BOSTON
401 Quincy St.
Dorchester, MA 02125
1-617-288-4182

NEW BEDFORD
556 County Rd.
New Bedford, MA 02740
1-508-997-7347

Michigan
DETROIT
P.O. Box 9260
Detroit, MI 48209
1-313-841-1394

Minnesota
MINNEAPOLIS
4528 401/2 Ave. N.
Robbinsdale, MN 55422
1-763-537-1125

Missouri
ST. LOUIS
3629 Cottage Ave.
St. Louis, MO 63113-3539
1-314-533-2777

New Jersey
ASBURY PARK
144 Ridge Ave.
Asbury Park, NJ 07712
1-732-775-1101

NEWARK
168 Sussex St.
Newark, NJ 07103
1-973-483-0165

New Mexico
CHICHILTAH
P.O. Box 267
Vanderwagen, NM 87326
1-505-778-5740

GALLUP
207 E. Wilson Ave.
Gallup, NM 87301
1-505-722-5261

New York
BROOKLYN
Queen of Hope
262 Macon St.
Brooklyn, NY 11216
1-718-453-7428

BRONX
Our Lady of the Immaculate Conception
335 E. 145th St.
Bronx, NY 10451
1-718-292-0019

HARLEM
406 West 127th St.
New York, NY 10027
1-212-222-7229

MANHATTAN
Gift of Love
657 Washington St.
New York, NY 10014
1-212-645-0587

North Carolina
CHARLOTTE
236 S. Torrence St.
Charlotte, NC 28204
1-704-344-8685

Pennsylvania
CHESTER
Gift of Mary
2714 West 9th St.
Chester, PA 19013
1-610-494-7424

NORRISTOWN
630 De Kalb St.
Norristown, PA 19401
1-610-277-5962

Tennessee
MEMPHIS
700 N. 7th St.
Memphis, TN 38107
1-901-527-4947

Texas
DALLAS
2704 Harlandale Ave.
Dallas, TX 75216
1-214-374-3351

HOUSTON
4703 Lelia St.
Houston, TX 77026
1-713-674-8282

Washington, D.C.
WASHINGTON, D.C. I
3310 Wheeler Rd. SE
Washington, D.C. 20032
1-202-562-6890

WASHINGTON, D.C. II
Gift of Peace
2800 Otis St., NE
Washington, D.C. 20018
1-202-269-3313

WASHINGTON, D.C. III
1646 Park Rd., N.W.
Washington, D.C. 20015
1-202-588-0091

Canada

MONTREAL
2465 Rue Champagne
Montreal, Quebec
Canada H2K 2G9
1-514-524-6372

ST. PAUL
4737 44th Ave.
St. Paul, Alberta
Canada TOA 3A3
1-780-645-2968

TORONTO
185 Dunn Ave.
Toronto, Ontario
Canada M6K 2S1
1-416-537-1391

VANCOUVER
2475 E. 48th Ave.
Vancouver, B.C.
Canada V5S 1G5
1-604-322-6840

WINNIPEG
167 Alkins St.
Winnipeg, Manitoba
Canada, R2W 4G1
1-204-582-2773

Mexico

TIJUANA-POSTAL
P.O. Box 2068
Imperial Beach, CA
91933
USA
52 664-682-5058

TIJUANA – EL
FLORIDO
P.O. Box 2068
Imperial Beach, CA
91933
USA
52-664-629-2484

TIJUANA—CENTRAL
P.O. Box 2068
Imperial Beach, CA
91933
USA
52 664-621-3041

APPENDIX 2 The Dr. Thomas A. Dooley Award

Established in 1984 by the University of Notre Dame Alumni Association, the Dr. Thomas A. Dooley Award annually recognizes a Notre Dame alumnus or alumna (living or deceased) for outstanding humanitarian service. The award honors Thomas A. Dooley III, a 1944 Notre Dame graduate and medical doctor who helped resettle North Vietnamese refugees in South Vietnam in the 1950s. In 1957, Dooley also founded MEDICO (the Medical International Cooperation Organization) to provide medical service and training to villagers in southeast Asia where medical care was minimal or nonexistent.

Dooley's best-selling books, *Deliver Us From Evil* (1955), *The Edge of Tomorrow* (1958), and *The Night They Burned the Mountain* (1960) told of his work with Laotian orphans and refugees fleeing Communism. He developed malignant melanoma in Laos and died back in the U.S. in January 1961. A bronze statue of Dooley with Laotian orphans stands near Notre Dame's Lourdes Grotto where he often prayed as a student. A small replica of the statue is given to each award recipient.

Dr. Paul A. Wright, M.D., won the Dr. Thomas A. Dooley Award in 2004 for humanitarian accomplishments. He founded the "Poorest of the Poor" project in the mid-1980s with his father to provide clothing, food, and supplies to the needy in impoverished areas in the U.S. and around the world. The program delivers 80,000 pounds of supplies to Appalachia each month. In 2001, he set up the "Medication Mission" program to provide free prescription drugs to needy people in northeastern Ohio. In its first year, the program supplied $800,000 worth of free medications.

Dr. Paul A. Wright, a 1972 graduate of the University of Notre Dame, receives the 2004 Dr. Thomas A. Dooley Award from Chuck Lennon, Executive Director of the Notre Dame Alumni Association.

Dr. Thomas A. Dooley Award Recipients

2005 – Sr. Joan Chittister, OSB '68 MA
2004 – Paul A. Wright, M.D. '72
2003 – James J. O'Connell, M.D. '70
2002 – Mary Brosnahan Sullivan '83
2001 – Angelo Capozzi, Jr., M.D. '56
2000 – John Adams '88

1999 – Erik G. Janowsky ’87 and
David Gaus, M.D. ’84
1998 – Robert Burke ’94
1997 – Kathleen M. Osberger ’75
1996 – Joseph L. Berry ’43
1995 – Rev. Louis J. Putz, CSC ’32
1994 – Louis M. Nanni ’84, ’88 M.A.
1998 – Robert Burke ’94
1997 – Kathleen M. Osberger ’75
1996 – Joseph L. Berry ’43
1995 – Rev. Louis J. Putz, CSC ’32
1994 – Louis M. Nanni ’84, ’88 M.A.
1993 – Julie K. O’Brien ’86 and
Sean P. O’Brien ’86 Arch
1992 – Dennis M. Nigro, M.D. ’69
1991 – Bro. William J. Tomes, Jr. ’59, ’62 M.A.
1990 – Alan P. Sondej ’74
1989 – Rev. Robert J. Lonbardo, OFM ’79
1988 – Cecilia H. Prinster ’76
1987 – Michael K. Novell ’75
1986 – Ann C. Titus ’80
1985 – Michael B. Bowler ’77

A native of Steubenville, Ohio, Paul A. Wright graduated from the University of Notre Dame in 1972. After medical school and a residency in cardiology, Paul began practicing in 1983, becoming a partner at the Ohio Heart Institute, a regional center for treating acute cardiac conditions.

Paul first met Mother Teresa in 1992, at a homeless shelter run by the Missionaries of Charity in Tijuana, Mexico. Mother Teresa was there recovering from a heart attack. Despite professional and financial success as a physician, Paul was anxious, depressed, empty. He feared that he was wasting his life and that God wasn't pleased with him.

Paul shared his concerns with Mother Teresa She told him to reread Matthew 25:35–46 where Jesus says that if we cared for the least of his brethren, "you did it for me." Mother Teresa told Paul to go home and live out this mandate. Paul visited some of her order's houses, including the House of the Dying in Calcutta. Seeing selfless compassion and service to the poorest of the poor transformed him. Though he served as a consulting cardiologist for Mother Teresa, "she cured me," Paul Wright insisted.

Paul returned to Ohio to live and practice medicine in a new way. In the 1980s, with his father, he founded the "Poorest of the Poor" program to distribute clothing, food and supplies to needy in the U.S. and in impoverished areas around the world. In 2001, he developed the "Medical Mission" program to provide free prescription drugs to northeastern Ohio residents who could not afford them. Paul and his wife Gayle live in Brookfild, Ohio and have one daughter, Maria Alana, a pre-school teacher.

A coworker of the Missionaries of Charity, Paul Wright attended beatification ceremonies for Mother Teresa in Rome in October 2003. This is his first book.

Founded in 1865, Ave Maria Press, a ministry of the Congregation of Holy Cross, is a Catholic publishing company that serves the spiritual and formative needs of the Church and its schools, institutions, and ministers; Christian individuals and families; and others seeking spiritual nourishment.